tiLes Gone Wild

NEW DIRECTIONS IN MIXED-MEDIA MOSAICS

Chrissie Grace

NORTH LIGHT BOOKS
CINCINNATI, OHIO
www.mycraftivity.com

12   11   10   09   08   5   4   3   2   1

Distributed in Canada by Fraser Direct
100 Armstrong Avenue
Georgetown, ON, Canada L7G 5S4
Tel: (905) 877-4411

Distributed in the U.K. and Europe by David & Charles
Brunel House, Newton Abbot, Devon, TQ12 4PU, England
Tel: (+44) 1626 323200, Fax: (+44) 1626 323319
E-mail: postmaster@davidandcharles.co.uk

Distributed in Australia by Capricorn Link
P.O. Box 704, S. Windsor, NSW 2756 Australia
Tel: (02) 4577-3555

Library of Congress Cataloging-in-Publication Data

Grace, Chrissie.
  Tiles gone wild : new directions in mixed-media mosaics / Chrissie Grace. -- 1st ed.
      p. cm.
  Includes bibliographical references and index.
  ISBN-13: 978-1-60061-081-3 (alk. paper)
  1. Mosaics--Technique. I. Title.
  TT910.G695 2008
  738.5--dc22

                    2008006566

Editor: Jennifer Claydon
Cover Designer: Marissa Bowers and Cheryl Mathauer
Interior Designer: Guy Kelly
Production Coordinator: Greg Nock
Photographers: Christine Polomsky, Ric Deliantoni
and Jim Carchidi
Stylist: Nora Martini

F+W PUBLICATIONS, INC.

www.fwpublications.com

Metric Conversion Chart

to convert	to	multiply by
Inches	Centimeters	2.54
Centimeters	Inches	0.4
Feet	Centimeters	30.5
Centimeters	Feet	0.03
Yards	Meters	0.9
Meters	Yards	1.1
Sq. Inches	Sq. Centimeters	6.45
Sq. Centimeters	Sq. Inches	0.16
Sq. Feet	Sq. Meters	0.09
Sq. Meters	Sq. Feet	10.8
Sq. Yards	Sq. Meters	0.8
Sq. Meters	Sq. Yards	1.2
Pounds	Kilograms	0.45
Kilograms	Pounds	2.2
Ounces	Grams	28.3
Grams	Ounces	0.035

DEDICATION

This book is dedicated to my father, who was unconditional in his love and support for me. This book is dedicated to you Dad:

Bob Mervine
March 14, 1947–October 16, 2007

Rest in Peace
I love you.

Photo by Chrissie Grace

ACKNOWLEDGMENTS

I would like to thank Tonia Davenport and North Light Books for choosing me to become a second-time author for them. I would also like to thank my editor, Jennifer Claydon, for many things: her endearing enthusiasm, her never-ending patience, her quick wit and sense of humor, her constant supply of afternoon chocolate and great taste in restaurants. Thanks for everything, Jenni! Last, thanks to Christine Polomsky, who I had the pleasure and privilege of working with again, and designers Marissa Bowers, Cheryl Mathauer and Guy Kelly.

ABOUT THE AUTHOR

Photo by Chrissie Grace

Chrissie Grace is a mixed-media mosaic artist and author of *Wild Tiles*, published by North Light Books in 2006. In addition to being a full-time mom, she is also a full-time artist. Chrissie's work is licensed in the stationery and gift industries, and she teaches workshops across the country.

Chrissie's work focuses on the whimsical and colorful aspects of life and shows the expansion of her creativity and her need to test limits. Her work is colorful and full of texture and substance, centering around inspirational themes.

Chrissie lives and works just outside of Orlando, Florida, with her lovely family. To learn more about Chrissie's work, visit her Web site at www.chrissiegrace. com. For daily inspiration, check out her blog at www.chrissiegrace.typepad.com.

Contents

Introduction

When I wrote *Wild Tiles* two years ago, I was an elementary school art teacher. Although I loved teaching, my heart ached to become a full-time artist and writer. With the support of my family and friends, and a big dose of courage, I took the leap of faith—and I have not been disappointed. Believing in myself strengthened my determination, expanded my creativity and widened my audience. I now have a career in the art licensing industry, and I love working for myself.

As I wrote this book and created projects for it, I aimed to break the boundaries of traditional mosaic work. I took a fresh approach to mosaics to create projects that will inspire you to try new things. Whether you are a seasoned artist with years of experience or a novice looking for inspiration for your first attempt at making mosaic art, the projects in this book are suitable for you. Several of them use traditional mosaic materials, such as tile, glass and smalti. However, many projects go off the beaten path, and I encourage you to experiment with paper, clay, bottle caps and handmade tesserae in your work. In mixed-media mosaics, when it comes to materials, the sky is the limit.

Aside from techniques, inspiration is the most important ingredient in making mixed-media mosaics. Inspiration comes to me in many forms; my children's laughter, a brand-new box of crayons or a favorite quote can move me to create a new piece. I also find so much inspiration from other artists, and the high-quality Web sites and blogs provided by artists today bring that inspiration straight to my home. Even the passing of my father last year, while very sorrowful, provided me with inspiration—to enjoy life to the fullest, to laugh more, to love more. The loss of him inspires me to make the most of every day.

Inspiration is what provides us with the innate desire to create. I believe that everyone has the desire to create something, whether it is a novel, a delicious pie, a comfortable home or an innovative product. If you are reading this book, then you must have the innate desire to create art. I urge you to record your inspiration; try writing down your thoughts, making lists of things that you are grateful for and sketching out ideas. Claim a space for yourself, even if it's in a closet or small corner, where you can create. Hang up a bulletin board and turn it into an Inspiration Board. Hang photos, quotes, magazine articles, fabric swatches and anything else that sparks your imagination. Have faith in your inspiration. Many people tell me that they come up with great ideas, but can't seem to execute their mosaics as they imagined. I always remind them: It's the journey that counts, not the destination. Don't be disappointed if a piece doesn't work out as you planned. You will learn something with every project you tackle. Everything in life is a work in progress—including you!

This book is written with the intention that you will learn many things and be inspired to make your own projects. I hope you find it informative, inspirational and, above all, fun! Please feel free to contact me through www.chrissiegrace.typepad.com with pictures of your completed projects. I would love to see your interpretations of the projects in this book. Thank you for taking this journey with me!

Chrissie Grace ⊚

"Never let the odds keep you from pursuing what you know in your heart you were meant to do."

— M. Jackson Brown, Jr.

Getting Started

Now that we've talked about getting inspired, it's time to actually get started! Because some of these projects veer off the path of traditional mosaics, it is very important to be familiar with the proper materials, tools and adhesives, so that your projects can be finished successfully.

Be prepared before beginning your project: Set up your work area, make sure you have all the necessary materials and supplies and review the steps for your project. Creating is a lot more fun when you have everything you need accessible and don't have to run around looking for supplies! And, of course, reference this section of the book as often as you need to while you're working.

"By failing to prepare, you are preparing to fail."

— Benjamin Franklin

MATERIALS

The materials that are used to make a mosaic are called tesserae. There is an excellent variety of commercial glass, tile and ceramic tesserae available today. Included in this section are all of the materials that we will use in this book, from classical mosaic materials to handmade mixed-media elements. Feel free to experiment with materials. I've seen mosaics made from flattened bottle caps and recycled clothing tags! When you are making mixed-media mosaics, possibilities for materials are endless.

Ceramic tile is an inexpensive and easily accessible material for mosaic tesserae that comes in a wide variety of colors, patterns and sizes. The most common ceramic tile size is 4" × 4" (10cm × 10cm). You can find ceramic tiles in home improvement stores. To create mosaic tesserae, ceramic tiles can be cut with a wet saw or broken with a hammer or tile nippers.

Smalti are the classic mosaic materials first used hundreds of years ago by Byzantine craftsmen. Available in a beautiful array of colors, smalti are small, thick, rectangular chunks of handmade glass. Smalti are more expensive than other mosaic materials. Mosaics made with smalti are rarely grouted.

Glass is a wonderful product to use in mosaics, and is available in a wide variety of forms. Stained glass is available in a rainbow of colors and can be purchased at a local stained glass supplier or online. I prefer to buy my stained glass in person because it makes color selection and matching easier, and it is cheaper than having the glass shipped. Tempered glass can also be used in mosaics, and shattered tempered glass creates a beautiful web pattern once grouted. Tempered glass can be found at most auto repair stores. One of my favorite decorative elements to use in mosaics is flat-backed glass marbles, which are available in rounds, squiggles and other shapes, such as stars. These are usually available at local craft stores, but can be found online as well.

Crockery can be a wonderful, unique addition to a mosaic. I love using crockery: broken pieces of mugs, cups, china, plates and bowls. They provide endless possibilities of colors, patterns and textures. The next time you accidentally break one of Grandma's antique teacups or your favorite coffee mugs save all of the broken pieces for tesserae! I like to pick up inexpensive pieces of crockery at thrift stores or garage sales as well.

Mixed-media elements include old jewelry pieces, board game pieces, beads, shells, buttons, beach glass, bottle caps and more. Using collected objects adds uniqueness and a sense of whimsy to your mosaics. Anything that can be glued down can be used. Some items, such as porous or fragile pieces, will need special attention to prevent damage when grouting.

Paper is a great decorative addition to a mosaic. Due to the popularity of scrapbooking, there is an incredible variety of beautiful papers available to artists today. Paper is easily accessible and does

not require any special safety attention. Handmade papers, construction paper, gift wrap and wallpaper all make great additions to a mixed-media mosaic. However, paper mosaics are decorative in nature and do not work well in functional areas, such as floors or anywhere outdoors.

Polymer clay can be sculpted into many different textures and shapes to create mosaic tesserae. It is also available in a large assortment of colors. Polymer clay needs to be baked, or cured, in a conventional oven before it can be used in a mosaic. Follow the manufacturer's instructions for preparation, safety and use of polymer clay.

Low-fire white clay can also be used to create handmade tesserae. You can create tesserae in any size, shape or design you desire by shaping the clay and then firing it. You can buy a small kiln for firing clay in your home or studio, or you can rent space in a kiln at a ceramics store.

Glazes and underglazes are used to color and decorate low-fire white clay before firing. You can expand your mosaic horizons even further by decorating your handmade tiles. I prefer to use underglazes because they can be used to create effects that glazes alone cannot achieve. Since underglazes don't melt during firing like glazes do, precise designs can be applied to clay tiles and they won't lose definition during firing. Underglazes always require a second firing with clear glaze to provide the sealing and durability qualities needed.

SURFACES

To assemble your mosaic, you will attach the tesserae you select to a base surface. Using the right adhesive and correct preparation can make almost anything a suitable surface for a mosaic.

A smooth, flat surface is the easiest to work with, but a little preparation can transform surfaces with various textures into the perfect bases for your mosaics.

Wood is the base surface for many of the projects in this book. Medium-density fiberboard (MDF) is the wood I prefer to use for most mosaics because it is available in varying thicknesses, is easy to cut with a jigsaw and has a smooth, consistent surface. Before adhering tesserae, prime MDF with a 1:4 solution of white craft glue and water. Please note that MDF is not weatherproof, and is therefore not suited for outdoor use. I also use thin plywood as a base for mosaics, and exterior-quality plywood is a good choice for outdoor mosaics, as it is water resistant. Both MDF and plywood are available at most home improvement stores.

Glass is the perfect surface to use for beautiful stained-glass mosaics because it allows light to shine through your mosaic, making it glow. You can also make interesting mosaics on shaped glass pieces, such as bottles and vases. When working with a glass base for a mosaic, be very careful to use a base that can support the weight of the tesserae without breaking. It is also important to use the appropriate adhesive when working with glass: Choose an adhesive that works on glass, and for stained-glass mosaics, use a clear adhesive or clear-drying adhesive so the mosaic remains transparent.

Furniture can be used as a mosaic base, which is an excellent way to recycle and create unique home décor. Select furniture that is sturdy enough to hold the weight of the tesserae. It is very important to properly prepare furniture to be the base for a mosaic. Sand off any old paint, thoroughly clean all of the surfaces, then prime the entire surface with a 1:4 solution of white craft glue and water. I have had the most success with doors, tables, chairs and dressers as mosaic bases.

Porous objects cannot be used as mosaic surfaces without special treatment because the glue will sink into the object, rather than staying on the surface and adhering the tesserae. Porous objects will also absorb grout. However, if you find a porous object with an interesting shape that you can't resist as a mosaic base, it can be made into a usable surface. Covering a porous item with aluminum tape creates a smooth surface suitable for a mosaic. Careful preparation will lead you to a successful project.

Other surfaces that can be used as the base of a mosaic are too numerous to count. Any smooth surface, or surface that can be treated to create a smooth surface, can be used. When planning a mosaic, carefully research the surface before starting so you know how to proceed for a successful project.

TOOLS AND SUPPLIES

It is essential that you have the correct tools and supplies when making mosaic artwork. Having all of the correct tools on hand will only make your life easier and your artwork better. Gather all your tools and materials before you begin working so that they are easy to reach while you work. You don't want to be stuck in the middle of a project searching for a missing tool! Listed below are all the tools and supplies you will need to begin. What you don't already have lying around your home can be found at your local home supply or craft store.

Tile nippers are probably the most important tool that I have in my mosaic toolbox. Used to cut tile and crockery into different shapes, tile nippers are essential to mosaic work. A high-quality pair should have tungsten-carbide edges for clean cuts. You can buy tile nippers at any home improvement store, as well as mosaic specialty shops. A good pair is worth its weight in gold!

Wheeled tile nippers are also used for cutting tile but can cut glass and other fragile materials as well. The wheels allow for more precise cuts than regular tile nippers. I use wheeled tile nippers primarily for cutting stained glass. Wheeled tile nippers can be found at home improvement stores and at mosaic or stained-glass specialty shops.

Ring blade saws cleanly cut all types of glass, tile, plastic and stone. If you are serious about mosaics, a ring blade saw is a wise investment. The blade is extremely sharp, can cut in any direction and also grinds while it cuts for smooth edges. This tool makes cutting curved pieces of glass very easy. Ring blade saws can be found at home improvement and stained-glass supply stores.

Glass scorers are useful tools when cutting glass by hand. The working end of the tool consists of a small hardened steel or carbide wheel. To use a glass scorer, roll the wheel across the glass along the line to be cut while applying considerable pressure. The pressure applied by the wheel does not cut the glass, but rather causes a small, localized, linear failure at the surface of the glass, resulting in a score line. The glass can then be easily broken right along the scored lines. Glass scorers can be found at home improvement stores and stained-glass specialty shops.

Running pliers are used to apply pressure to glass in order to break it along score lines. You can find running pliers at stained-glass specialty shops.

Hammers can be used to break large objects or thick pieces of tesserae that are too big for tile nippers. To keep shards from flying around, place objects beneath an old towel before breaking them with a hammer.

A jigsaw (also called a saber saw) cuts in a rapid up-and-down motion. Jigsaws are ideal for cutting curves and complex shapes in wood. Jigsaws work best for cutting wood that is no more than 1½" (4cm) thick. When using a jigsaw, always use a sharp blade and follow all safety precautions. Work in a well-ventilated area and wear safety goggles and a dust mask. Jigsaws are available at home improvement stores.

Safety goggles protect your eyes while you work; things like the sharp shards created when nipping glass or tile, grout dust and more pose risks to your eyes. Wearing safety goggles is a very important part of safety procedures.

Carbon transfer paper is a great way to transfer images onto wood. To use carbon paper, print images to the desired size, sandwich the transfer paper between the design and the wood, and trace the design with a pencil.

Tweezers give you more control when working with tesserae that are hard to handle. They are convenient for picking up small tesserae and putting them in tight spaces.

Adhesives are very important to the finished strength and quality of a mosaic. It is important to choose the correct adhesive for your projects. When working on outdoor projects, use a cement-based adhesive that is frost- and waterproof. To adhere mirrors, a clear silicone sealant is ideal because it won't eat away at the silver backing. To re-create most of the mosaics in this book, you can use tile mastic or clear silicone sealant. I recommend buying Weldbond tile adhesive. It is by far my favorite tile adhesive. It is nontoxic, dries clear and holds up very well. Weldbond is available at various online mosaic supply stores and most craft stores.

Grout enhances the overall look of the final piece and supports, frames and protects the tesserae. There are two types of grout:

sanded and unsanded. For all of the grouted projects in this book, use sanded grout, which is available at any home improvement store. Unsanded grout can only be used for openings that are ⅛" (3mm) or smaller. In larger openings, this type of grout will crack and be difficult to smooth. Grout comes in a variety of colors, but can also be mixed with acrylic paint to create additional colors. See page 18 for more information on using grout.

Two-part epoxy resin can be used as an alternative to grout and is especially attractive on stained-glass projects. Epoxy resin is available in most craft stores. See page 20 for more information on working with epoxy resin.

Buckets of various sizes can be used for mixing grout. After using a bucket for grout, clean it outside when you're done, because grout can clog drains and cause serious damage.

Gloves are extremely important to use while grouting a mosaic. They protect your hands from staining, drying out and, most importantly, from being cut by sharp tesserae. I recommend surgical gloves or dishwashing gloves.

Filter masks are another very important safety precaution. Always wear a filter mask when mixing grout and when cleaning grout off of a mosaic to prevent breathing in harmful dust particles.

Painter's tape is the best product I've found to protect different surfaces from paint or grout. It is easy to put on a project and the adhesive doesn't damage surfaces when the tape is pulled off. Painter's tape is available in varying widths and can be found at hardware stores.

A dustpan and brush should be kept in your work area for quick cleanups. Sharp tile and glass shards left on the ground or on a work tabletop can be very dangerous and should be cleaned up after every stage of a project.

Cloths and sponges, including old towels, discarded T-shirts and old baby burp cloths, are handy for wiping down grout and pol-

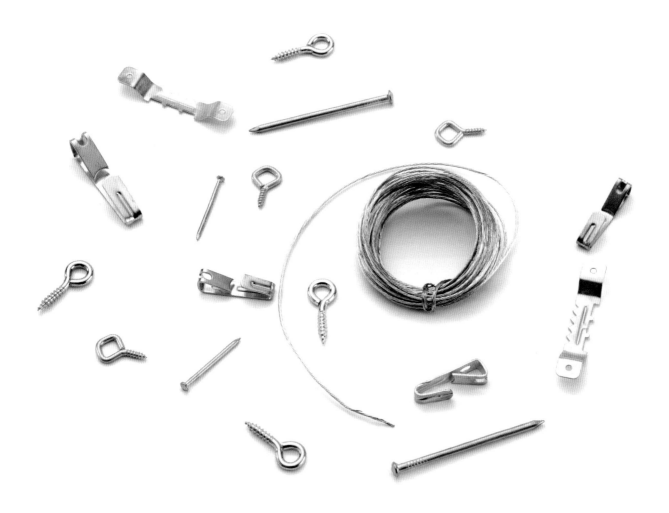

ishing finished mosaics. Cut large cloths into small square pieces for convenience.

Acrylic paints are a colorful, simple way to finish off the edges of a mosaic. I also like to use acrylic paints to tint grout. Acrylic paint is inexpensive, comes in a wide variety of colors and is easy to find at most craft stores.

Sealants protect a finished mosaic. I suggest sealing wood with diluted craft glue and sealing grout with a grout sealer, especially for outdoor projects. Polyacrylic sealants dry clear and provide a protective finish for porous items, such as wooden game pieces or shells, which you may wish to include in your mosaic. Use a polymer clay sealant on polymer clay pieces included in a mosaic.

Hanging hardware is attached to a mosaic so that it can be hung like the work of art that it is. Covering the back of a mosaic with brown paper is an optional step that gives a mosaic a professional look. My preferred pieces of hanging hardware are screw eyes

and metal wire. See page 19 for more information on preparing a mosaic for hanging.

A rolling pin is a tool that you will find useful for rolling out clay. A slab roller produces a more even, accurate slab, but it is also more expensive. For rolling low-fire white clay, I prefer to use wooden rolling pins.

Craft knives are useful for many general hobby tasks. For mosaics, craft knives are used to cut clay into handmade tiles and to trim backing paper when preparing a mosaic for hanging.

A kiln is a specialized oven used to fire clay and other materials at very high temperatures. Unless ceramics is a very serious hobby or business for you, a small hobby ceramic kiln will probably suit your needs. To fire the low-fire white clay used in the following projects, you will need access to a top- or front-loading kiln that fires up to 2372° F (1300° C). If you don't want to invest in your own kiln, most pottery stores will fire your pieces for you for a small fee.

Techniques

Techniques are of utmost importance when making mosaics. Although creativity and ingenuity are essential to a striking mosaic piece, correct technique is essential to successfully completing your work of art. Mistakes are inevitable when you are starting out or trying new things, but with just a little practice you'll be amazed at how comfortable you can feel with these skills. Always remember when using any of these techniques to work carefully and follow all safety instructions.

NIPPING TILE

Nipping tiles is one technique that you will soon consider second nature as a mosaic artist. If you are a beginner, don't be intimidated by the use of tile nippers. Use inexpensive tiles that are available at home improvement stores for practice. Always nip tile over an old towel or newspaper to catch any shards or stray pieces and wear safety goggles to protect your eyes.

1 Begin cutting
Make the first cut halfway down one side of the tile. Place the edge of the tile inside the cutting area of the tile nippers and squeeze firmly. The tile will break into two pieces.

2 Continue cutting
Repeat Step 1 to cut each tile fragment into smaller pieces.

3 Trim tiles to correct size
Continue cutting the tile fragments with tile nippers until they are the size needed for the mosaic. When cutting small tiles, hold the tiles along the edges and be very careful not to cut your fingers.

4 Shape tiles (optional)
Use wheeled tile nippers to create tesserae with straight edges. For triangles, cut tile into squares, and then cut the squares diagonally with wheeled tile nippers.

CREATING GLASS TESSERAE

Cutting glass is another technique that may seem intimidating, but it really is quite easy and safe if you follow the proper procedure. If you give the glass a good score, it will break easily and cleanly.

Keep the glass scorer filled with lubricating oil to keep the blade moving freely. Wear safety goggles, and if you worry about cutting yourself, wear thin surgical gloves to protect your hands.

1 Score glass

Place the glass securely on a protective cover on top of your work surface. Using a straightedge (I prefer using a cork-backed metal ruler), press the scoring tool firmly on the glass and score.

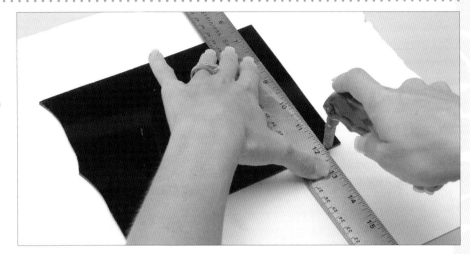

2 Break glass

Insert the glass into the running pliers, lining up the center mark on the running pliers with the score mark on the glass. Gently squeeze the pliers shut to break the glass on the score.

3 Create tiles

To cut glass into small tiles, either repeat Steps 1 and 2 or use wheeled tile nippers on the glass strips.

CREATING CLAY TILES

I like to use a low-fire white clay to create my own clay tiles and tesserae. Clay opens up the world of mosaics to an unlimited variety of possibilities. You can cut clay to any shape or size that you want, and you can create a never-ending selection of textures as well. The huge color selection of underglazes only increases the possibilities. Creating your own clay tiles will help you design unique, one-of-a-kind pieces.

1 Roll clay
Cover your work surface with shiny-side-up wax paper to protect it. Roll low-fire white clay to ¼" (6mm) thickness, using a rolling pin or slab roller.

2 Cut clay
Using a template or straightedge as a guide, cut the rolled clay with a craft knife.

3 Smooth edges
Allow the clay to dry to leather hardness. Smooth all of the cut edges with a damp sponge.

4 Apply underglaze
Dry the clay pieces overnight. Apply 2 to 3 coats of underglaze to the dried clay. Often, the color of the liquid or dried underglaze is not the color it will be after firing. So when picking an underglaze color, make sure to refer to the manufacturer's chart to see the color it will be after it is fired.

5 Decorate tiles (optional)
Once the underglaze base is dry, apply additional colors of underglaze to decorate the clay as desired. A squeeze bottle with a small tip can be used to achieve fine lines and details. Allow the underglazes to completely dry and fire tiles according to manufacturer's instructions.

6 Apply clear glaze
Allow the tiles to cool completely after firing. Apply 2 coats of clear glaze to the fired tiles. The clear glaze will appear bluish before firing, but it will be clear after firing. Fire the tiles according to the manufacturer's instructions.

TRANSFERRING A PATTERN

There are a few different ways to transfer patterns, but my preferred method is to use carbon transfer paper. It is available in white or charcoal; white works best for dark surfaces and charcoal works best for light surfaces. The paper can be reused quite a few times before the carbon is worn off.

1 Trace pattern over carbon paper

Lay a piece of carbon transfer paper over an MDF or plywood panel. Lay the mosaic pattern on top of the carbon transfer paper. Using a pencil, trace over the lines of the mosaic pattern, pressing firmly.

2 Trace pattern with permanent marker

Go over the transferred lines with a permanent marker to make the pattern easier to see as you work.

USING A JIGSAW

Some people are easily intimidated by power tools, but don't be. As long as you are careful and follow the manufacturer's safety instructions, jigsaws are not difficult to use. Jigsaws are an excellent way to shape your mosaic base. Learning to use one will really open up the possibilities for your mosaic designs. Remember to wear eye protection, as well as a mask to filter out dust particles. Secure loose clothing and long hair, and keep the power cord out of the way of the blade as you're working.

1 Cut surface

Transfer the mosaic pattern to the surface. Before cutting, read the instruction manual for your equipment thoroughly and follow all manufacturer's instructions. Wear eye protection and secure your hair as well as any loose clothing or jewelry. Place the wood on a safe work surface and secure it before cutting. Keep the wood secure as you cut along the marked lines, turning the wood as needed. Take your time and work carefully to avoid injury to yourself or damage to your tools or surface.

2 Sand edges

When you have finished cutting the wood, sand the rough edges.

USING GROUT

Grouting is a messy but necessary part of mosaics. When you are working with grout, work in a well-ventilated area that can be cleaned easily, and always wear gloves to protect your hands from sharp tesserae. As discussed in Tools and Supplies on page 12, use sanded grout for all of the grouted projects in this book. Remember that grout is like concrete, and it will be very hard to clean off of the tesserae if it dries too much too soon.

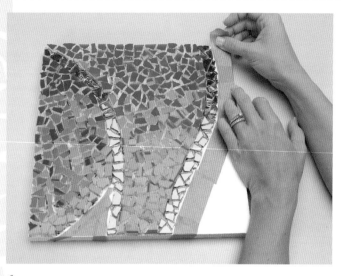

1 Prepare mosaic

Before grouting a mosaic, allow the tile adhesive to dry completely. Make sure to scrape any dried glue off of the tops of the tiles. Tape off the sides of the panel and any painted areas with painter's tape.

2 Mix grout

Use the manufacturer's guidelines to determine the amount of grout and water to mix. Follow the instructions for mixing the grout. Slowly add water, stirring vigorously to combine the water and grout. Add more grout or water as needed to reach a consistency a little thicker than pancake batter.

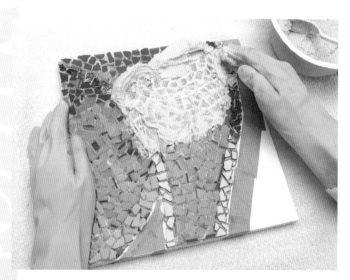

3 Spread grout

Lay a large spot of grout on the mosaic, then spread it over the surface, pushing the grout into all of the spaces between the tesserae. Be careful of sharp edges on the tesserae. Spread grout over the entire surface of the mosaic until all of the spaces are filled.

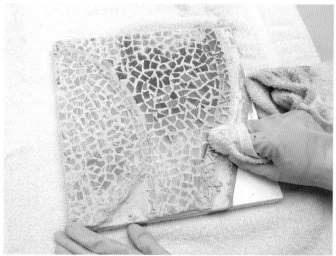

4 Clean tiles

Allow the grout to dry until it is set. This takes approximately 10 minutes, but temperature and humidity will affect drying time. Use a damp towel or sponge to wipe the excess grout off of the surface of the tiles, taking care not to pull grout from between the tesserae. Be careful that your wiping material is not too wet; excess moisture will cause the grout to start spreading again. Once the surface is smooth, buff the tesserae with a clean towel.

PREPARING A MOSAIC FOR HANGING

Mosaics can be quite heavy, and you should never create a safety problem by suspending a large mosaic from a small nail or picture hanger. Mosaic artwork needs to be securely anchored. Pieces weigh-ing more than fifty pounds should be anchored to the studs in the wall for safety. Make sure to properly insert the hooks and attach wire so that you don't have to worry about your piece falling.

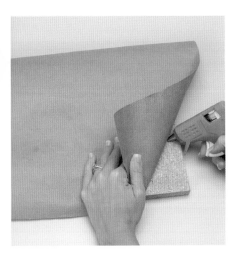

1 Adhere paper backing

Cut a piece of brown paper that is larger than the surface you will be covering. Adhere the paper to the back of the mosaic with a hot glue gun.

2 Trim paper backing

Once the glue has set, turn the mosaic over and use a craft knife to trim the brown backing paper to the same size as the mosaic.

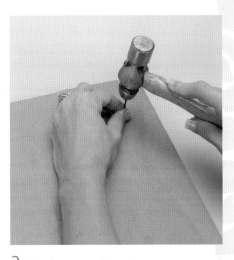

3 Mark screw locations

Using a straightedge and a pencil, mark the backing for the placement of the screw eyes. The placement of the screws depends on the size, shape and weight of the finished piece. Make a hole for each screw by pounding a thin nail ¼" (6mm) into the MDF board at the marked locations. Remove the nails from the MDF board.

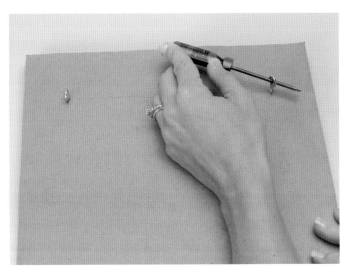

4 Attach screws

Twist a screw eye into each nail hole. To aid in turning the screw, insert a small screwdriver through the eye of the screw for leverage.

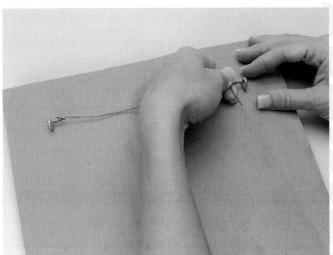

5 Attach hanging wire

Insert the end of a piece of steel galvanized wire through the screw eye, leaving a 2" (5cm) tail. Twist the wire tail around the remaining wire to secure it. Repeat on the other side.

USING A TWO-PART EPOXY RESIN

Two-part epoxy resin is composed of an epoxy and a hardener. Once the two are mixed together, they form a material that has a very strong bond when cured. It is essential when using two-part epoxy to follow all safety precautions; make sure to read and follow the manufacturer's safety instructions. When the epoxy resin is in liquid form, it can be a skin and eye irritant. Once the epoxy has cured, most types are nontoxic and do not irritate the skin. Make sure to wear safety gloves and goggles, and always work in a well-ventilated area. Handle the liquid with care, and be sure to dispose of the left-over materials properly, as recommended by the manufacturer.

1 Protect project bottom

To protect the back of the project from excess drips of epoxy, cover it with a piece of contact paper.

2 Elevate project

Lay down a layer of wax paper to protect your work surface. Place the project on disposable cups over the wax paper.

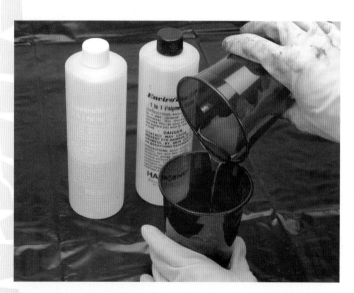

3 Measure the resin and hardener

Following the manufacturer's instructions, measure out the amount of hardener you will need to cover the project into one disposable cup. Measure an equal amount of resin into a second cup. Pour the resin into the hardener.

4 Mix epoxy

Using a craft stick, vigorously stir the resin and hardener together until thoroughly blended. Scrape the sides and bottom of the cup as you stir to integrate the two. Pour the mixture into the cup that held the measured resin and continue stirring until there are enough bubbles in the mixture to resemble champagne.

5 Pour mixture

Pour the epoxy over the surface of the project. Start in the center and work toward the edges in a circular pattern.

6 Spread epoxy

Spread the epoxy with a craft stick to cover the entire surface of the piece in an even layer. Work from the center outward, allowing any excess coating to run off the edges of the piece.

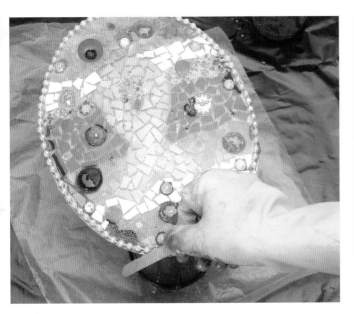

7 Clean edges

Once the epoxy is spread over the top surface of the piece, scrape the edges with a craft stick to eliminate any drips.

8 Eliminate air bubbles

Allow the epoxy to set up for about 10 minutes. As the air bubbles rise to the surface, get rid of them by passing an embossing heat tool over the surface. The carbon dioxide in the air blown by the embossing heat tool will pop the bubbles. Keep the tip of the embossing tool at least 3" (8cm) from the surface of the piece and keep it in constant motion.

Allow the epoxy to completely cure, following the manufacturer's guidelines. After the epoxy has cured, remove the protective backing from the piece.

Getting Clever with Clay

MOST MOSAICS ARE MADE FROM EXISTING COMMERCIAL tiles or glass. But the mosaics in this chapter are not most mosaics: They all feature handmade tesserae created using low-fire white clay. Making your own tesserae provides you with endless freedom and flexibility. The most important advantage to using clay to create tesserae is that you can shape it into any form you desire. For example, if you want to make a mosaic that features a heart, you don't have to just fill one in with broken tiles. You can make a heart tile out of clay in any size, shape and color you wish! This gives your mosaics a more unique, eclectic look.

There are many ways to give your handmade clay tesserae an interesting appearance. Stamps pressed into the clay can provide interesting textures or poignant messages. A rolling pin can be used to press textured items, such as doilies, into the clay. Three-dimensional tesserae can be created by layering pieces of clay. To cut clay into tiles, use a sharp craft knife for freehand cutting, or try cookie cutters for repeatable shapes. Once the clay is textured and cut, you can decorate your tiles with underglazes to create your own miniature works of art.

From choosing words or symbols that are inspirational to you, as in *Inspiration Squared* on page 24, to designing your own color palette for a project like *Puzzle Pieces* on page 32, the sky is the limit with handmade clay tiles. After trying out the projects in this book, see what inspires you. Try designing your own clay tiles to see what your creative mind comes up with!

"Imagination is the beginning of creation. You imagine what you desire, you will what you imagine, and at last you create what you will."

– George Bernard Shaw

Inspiration Squared

THIS PIECE IS MEANT TO BE FUN, WHIMSICAL AND FULL of inspiration. I believe in the power of positive thoughts and affirmations, and I like to surround myself with positive messages and bright colors. This project brings all of those things together.

To create your own inspirational mosaic, pick seven or eight words that make you feel good. For my own squares, I chose *wish, prayer, inspire, believe, love, dream* and *give*. If these words don't speak to your heart, choose some others. Some other inspirational words include: *dance, sing, hope, power, family, friends, grow, imagine, travel, adventure, care* and *fly*. Of course, there are millions to choose from.

This project would make a great gift for someone you love, or for yourself. Hang it somewhere you'll see it often and smile.

"The future belongs to those who believe in the beauty of their dreams."

— Eleanor Roosevelt

Materials

10" × 13" (25cm × 33cm) MDF panel

Low-fire white clay

Underglazes in the following colors: black, white, red, orange, yellow, green, light blue, dark blue, purple and pink

Clear glaze

Tile adhesive

Black grout

Black acrylic paint

Wax paper

White craft glue

Pencil

Rolling pin or slab roller

Craft knife

Sponge

Assortment of paintbrushes

Squeeze bottle with small tip

Access to a kiln

Tile nippers

Painter's tape

Brown paper backing

Hot glue gun and glue sticks

2 screw eyes

10" (25cm) length of 20-gauge steel galvanized wire

Hammer

Clean towel

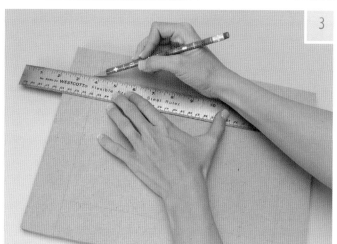
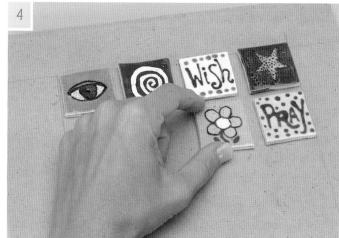

1 Prepare clay

Cover your work surface with wax paper to protect it. Roll low-fire white clay to ¼" (6mm) thickness, using a rolling pin or slab roller. Using a craft knife, cut out 24 2" (5cm) squares from the clay. Cut the uneven edges from the remaining clay scraps. The scrap clay will be used to create the border tiles.

Let all the clay pieces dry until leather hard, then use a wet sponge to smooth out any rough edges. Allow the clay pieces to dry overnight. Paint all of the clay scraps with 2 to 3 coats of white underglaze, and then add dots with black underglaze.

2 Fire tiles

Paint each tile with 2 to 3 basecoats of underglaze. After the tiles have dried, draw images and words on the tiles in pencil.

The pencil marks will fire off in the kiln. Decorate your designs with underglazes.

Fire all of the tiles and scraps following the manufacturer's instructions. After the tiles have cooled, apply a clear glaze to each tile. Fire the pieces again following the manufacturer's instructions. After this firing, the clay tiles will be shiny and non-porous (see Creating Clay Tiles, page 16).

3 Prepare board

Prepare the surface of the wood by mixing a 1:4 solution of craft glue and water. Paint the solution on the surface and let dry. Mark a 1½" (4cm) border around the edge of the MDF panel.

4 Begin mosaic

Using the marked frame as a guide, begin adhering the square clay tiles to the MDF panel using tile adhesive. For a precise, geometric mosaic, mark a grid on the wood and follow it when placing the clay tiles. For a more organic look, eyeball the placement of each square.

◎ Wild Idea

When adding fine details or text to a clay tile, try using a squeeze bottle with a fine tip instead of a paintbrush to apply the underglaze. This will give you more control over the flow of the underglaze, and a small tip will create fine, neat lines.

5 Create border

Use tile nippers to break up the black-and-white clay tiles. Fill in the border with the black-and-white tesserae.

6 Grout mosaic

Allow the tile adhesive to dry completely. Tape off the sides of the MDF panel with painter's tape, then grout the piece with black grout. Clean the tiles when the grout has set. Once the surface is smooth, buff the tesserae with a clean towel (see Using Grout, page 18).

7 Paint edges

Allow the grout to dry completely. Remove the painter's tape and paint the edges of the MDF panel with black acrylic paint.

8 Prepare mosaic for hanging

Once the paint has dried, cover the back of the MDF panel with brown paper backing. Attach 2 screw eyes to the back of the piece, 2" (5cm) in from the top edge and 1½" (4cm) in from the sides. Add wire to hang (see Preparing a Mosaic for Hanging, page 19).

5

6

7

8

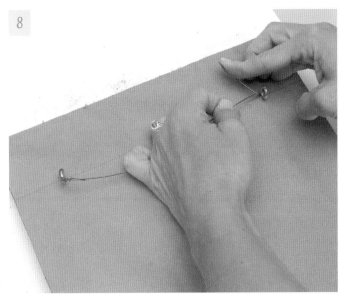

Art Is Life

FRIDA KAHLO HAS ALWAYS BEEN ONE OF MY FAVORITE artists, as well as a huge inspiration. She lived a difficult life and used her art and constant self-portraits as a means of art therapy. Frida Kahlo was a beautiful woman inside and out. I believe for her that Art meant Life, hence the title of the project based on my admiration for the artist and her artwork.

I used a bright palette to correspond with traditional colors in Mexican artwork and to contrast with the skulls, which are included to represent El Dia de los Muertos, or Day of the Dead, a Mexican holiday that honors and celebrates loved ones who have died.

As you work on this project, think of someone you admire. What quotes or images would you use to create a tribute piece? Who are you inspired to honor and celebrate?

"I paint my own reality. The only thing I know is that I paint because I need to, and I paint whatever passes through my head without any other consideration."

— Frida Kahlo

Materials

Pattern (page 118)

12" × 24" (30cm × 61cm) MDF panel

Low-fire white clay

Underglazes in the following colors: flesh, light blue, black, white, red, orange, yellow and purple

Clear glaze

Tile adhesive

20 pieces black smalti

20 pieces white smalti

Gray grout

Black acrylic paint

Wax paper

Carbon transfer paper

White craft glue

Pencil

Rolling pin or slab roller

Craft knife

Small star- and flower-shaped cookie cutters

Sponge

Assortment of paintbrushes

Squeeze bottle with small tip

Access to a kiln

Tile nippers

Painter's tape

Brown paper backing

Hot glue gun and glue sticks

2 screw eyes

12" (30cm) length of 20-gauge steel galvanized wire

Hammer

Towel

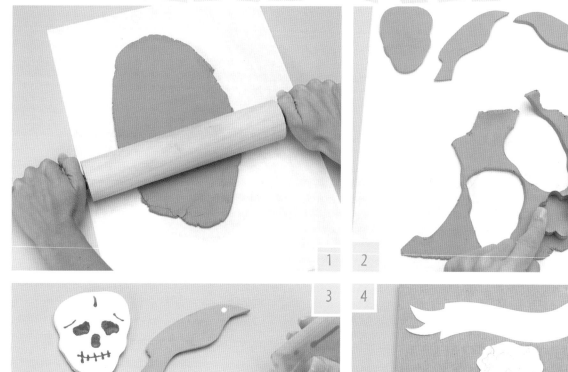

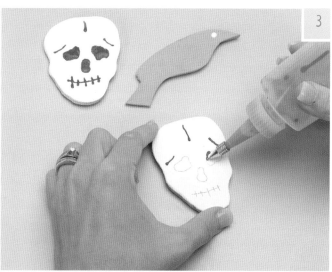

1 Prepare clay

Cover your work surface with wax paper (shiny side up) to help protect it. Roll your low-fire white clay to ¼" (6mm) thickness using a rolling pin or slab roller. Transfer the pattern on page 118 onto a piece of paper (see Transferring a Pattern, page 17). Cut out each pattern piece.

2 Cut clay pieces

Lay the pattern pieces on the clay and lightly trace around them with a pencil, indenting the clay. Use a craft knife to cut out the clay pieces following the marks in the clay. Cut 20 clay stars with the star-shaped cookie cutter and 6 clay flowers with the flower-shaped cookie cutter. Gather the remaining clay scraps and roll the clay out again to ¼" (6mm) thickness. Cut the clay sheet into strips—these will be used to create the blue background tiles.

3 Finish clay tiles

Let all of the clay pieces dry to leather hardness and use a wet sponge to smooth out any rough edges. Paint each tile with 2 to 3 basecoats of underglaze in the appropriate color. Use a squeeze bottle filled with the black underglaze to write "Art Is Life" in the banner, and to fill in the fine details on the other clay pieces. Fire all of the tiles following the manufacturer's instructions. After the tiles have cooled, apply a clear glaze to each tile. Fire the pieces again following the manufacturer's instructions. After this firing, the clay tiles will be shiny and nonporous (see Creating Clay Tiles, page 16).

4 Transfer pattern

Prepare the surface of the wood by mixing a 1:4 solution of craft glue and water. Paint the solution on the surface and let dry. Transfer the pattern on page 118 to the MDF panel.

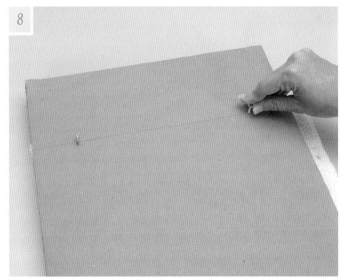

5 Begin mosaic

Use tile nippers to break up the light blue clay tiles. Using tile adhesive, fill in the background of the piece with a combination of blue tesserae, stars and flowers. Continue adding black and white smalti tiles until the design is finished, making sure the mosaic is filled and there are no gaps.

6 Grout mosaic

Allow the tile adhesive to dry completely. Tape off the sides of the MDF panel with painter's tape, then grout the piece with gray grout. Clean the tiles when the grout has set. Once the surface is smooth, buff the tesserae with a clean towel (see Using Grout, page 18).

7 Paint edges

Allow the grout to dry completely. Remove the painter's tape and paint the edges of the MDF panel with black acrylic paint.

8 Prepare mosaic for hanging

Once the paint has dried, cover the back of the MDF panel with brown paper backing. Attach 2 screw eyes to the back of the piece, 4" (10cm) in from the top edge and 2" (5cm) in from the sides. Add wire to hang (see Preparing a Mosaic for Hanging, page 19).

◎ Wild Idea

For easy cleanup, I like to do all of my grouting on top of inexpensive plastic tablecloths. They are large enough to cover my entire work surface and when I am done, I just roll them up and toss them out, and all of the mess is gone.

Puzzle Pieces

EVERY MOSAIC IS LIKE A PUZZLE. YOU BREAK UP THE tiles, and then you fit them back together to create a new picture. I think that mosaics and puzzles are both great metaphors for life. When our lives fall apart, as they sometimes do, we pick up the pieces and put everything back together.

This project brings these metaphors even closer together by using puzzle pieces made from clay. Follow the template provided and personalize your own project by changing the color of the glazes, or create your own puzzle pattern for an original piece.

This mosaic also has the added feature of painted grout. I painted the grout here to add a beautiful metallic element, but you can paint the grout of any mosaic, either to achieve a bolder color than mixing paint with grout, or to fix up a project that didn't come out quite right.

Materials

Pattern (page 124)

12" × 12" (30cm × 30cm) wooden frame

4" × 4" (10cm × 10cm) mirror

Low-fire white clay

Underglazes in the following colors: turquoise, dark blue, red, purple, pink, white and black

Clear glaze

10 large, clear flat-backed glass marbles

Acrylic paints in white and black

Watercolor paper or white cardstock

White grout

Silver leaf paint

20 small nails

Black polymer clay

2 squeeze bottles with small tips

Painter's tape

Clear craft glue

Silicone adhesive

White craft glue

Pencil

Carbon transfer paper

Rolling pin or slab roller

Craft knife

Sponge

Assortment of paintbrushes

Access to a kiln

Wax paper

2 screw eyes

12" (30cm) length of 20-gauge steel galvanized wire

Hammer

"There are no extra pieces in the universe. Everyone is here because he or she has a place to fill, and every piece must fit itself into the big jigsaw puzzle."

— Deepak Chopra

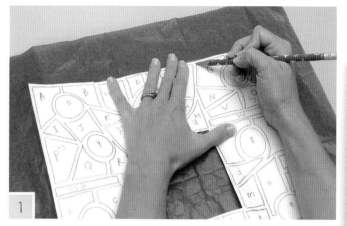

1 Prepare frame

Prepare the surface of the wood by mixing a 1:4 solution of craft glue and water. Paint the solution on the surface and let dry. Transfer the pattern on page 124 onto a piece of paper, then onto the frame using carbon tracing paper (see Transferring a Pattern, page 17). Carefully label each area of the pattern.

2 Cut clay

Cut the mosaic pieces out of the paper pattern. Cover your work surface with wax paper, shiny side up, to protect it. Roll low-fire white clay to ¼" (6mm) thickness, using a rolling pin or slab roller. Lay the pattern pieces on the clay and lightly trace around them with a pencil, indenting the clay. Use a craft knife to cut out the clay pieces following the marks in the clay. Mark the back of each piece to match your pattern so you can easily identify the pieces later.

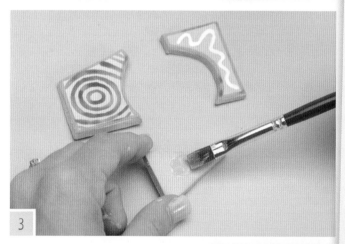

3 Finish clay tiles

Let all of the clay pieces dry to leather hardness and use a wet sponge to smooth out any rough edges. Paint each tile with 2 to 3 basecoats of underglaze in the appropriate color. Use squeeze bottles filled with black and white underglaze to fill in the fine details on the clay pieces. Fire all of the tiles following the manufacturer's instructions. After the tiles have cooled, apply a clear glaze to each tile. Fire the pieces again following the manufacturer's instructions. After this firing, the clay tiles will be shiny and non-porous (see Creating Clay Tiles, page 16).

4 Decorate marbles

Using acrylic paint, paint 4 black 1½" (4cm) squares and 6 white 1½" (4cm) squares on a piece of white cardstock or watercolor paper. Using the end of a paintbrush, add dots of white acrylic paint to the black squares and dots of black acrylic paint to the white squares. After the paint has dried, use clear craft glue to adhere the marbles to the paper. Allow the glue to dry, then carefully trim the paper around the marbles.

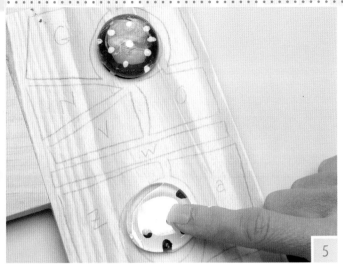

5 Begin mosaic

Using the pattern as a guide, glue the paper-backed marbles to the frame, and then glue the clay puzzle pieces around them. This particular mosaic has a larger grout line than normal, so don't be alarmed if the pieces look like they are spaced a little too widely. Make sure to allow at least 24 hours for the mosaic to dry.

6 Paint grout

Tape the sides of the frame with painter's tape, then grout the piece using white grout (see Using Grout, page 18). Try to keep the grout level with the larger grout lines. Clean the frame once the grout has set. Remove the painter's tape. Allow the grout to dry completely. Using a paintbrush with a fine tip, very carefully paint the grout lines using silver leaf paint and let them dry completely.

7 Create polymer clay spheres

Roll the black polymer clay into 20 ½" (1cm) spheres. Press the head of a nail halfway into each of the spheres, leaving a hole. Bake the polymer clay following the manufacturer's instructions. Allow the clay to cool completely.

8 Finish frame

Pound 5 nails into each side of the frame, 2" (5cm) apart. Glue the polymer clay spheres onto the nails. Secure the mirror to the frame using silicone adhesive. Attach 2 screw eyes to the back of the piece, 2" (5cm) in from the top edge and 2" (5cm) in from the sides. Add wire to hang (see Preparing a Mosaic for Hanging, page 19).

◎ Wild Idea

I left wider grout lines in this project with the intention of painting the grout. Although it is possible to create many different colors of grout by adding acrylic paint, this is the best way I have found to emulate a metallic grout.

Reach *for* the *Stars*

Materials

Patterns (page 121)

Text-weight paper

36" × 5" (91cm × 13cm) MDF panel

6" × 6" (15cm × 15cm) MDF panel

3" × 5" (8cm × 13cm) plywood panel

3" × 8½" (8cm × 22cm) plywood panel

6" × 23½" (15cm × 60cm) plywood panel

Low-fire white clay

Underglazes in the following colors: brown, white, black and blue

Clear glaze

1 large, clear flat-backed glass marble

5" (13cm) polystyrene foam ball

Aluminum tape

Plastic heart (packaging from candy shown here)

4" × 4" (10cm × 10cm) ceramic tiles in black and red

Stained glass in the following colors: clear, iridescent white, white, red, turquoise, yellow and lavender

Purple smalti

Mirror

Acrylic paints in the following colors: black, white and lavender

Gold leaf paint

White grout

Black grout

White craft glue

Silicone adhesive

Clear permanent glue

Painter's tape

Tile adhesive

Carbon transfer paper

Jigsaw or scroll saw

Sandpaper

Pencil

Rolling pin or slab roller

Craft knife

Sponge

Assortment of paintbrushes

Access to a kiln

Computer and printer

Wheeled tile nippers

Glass scorer

Running pliers

Towel

2 screw eyes

6" (15cm) length of 20-gauge steel galvanized wire

Hammer

Give Yourself Wings

THIS PROJECT IS VERY PERSONAL TO ME BECAUSE IT USES symbols that I find meaningful. However, I think that many people can relate to this message. This piece is about the journey to find one's true self. It is meant to be an altar and should be hung in a very special place.

The eye symbolizes recognizing the truth in all things, because I believe truth is the cornerstone of all happiness and inner peace. The key and lock symbolize the act of opening the lock on one's proverbial heart. We have all been hurt at one point or another and may be tempted to lock our hearts away, but it is essential to allow love in. The roof at the top of the altar symbolizes the way our bodies house our spirits and souls. The wings are a symbol of flight, and the words speak for themselves.

This project is a great example of a mixed-media mosaic. From tiles and handmade clay pieces to plastic candy holders and polystyrene foam balls, the materials are as unique and eclectic as the finished project.

"Will today be the day you decide once and for all to make your life consistent with the quality of your spirit? Then start by proclaiming, 'This is what I am. This is what my life is about. And this is what I'm going to do. Nothing will stop me from achieving my destiny. I will not be denied!'"

– Anthony Robbins

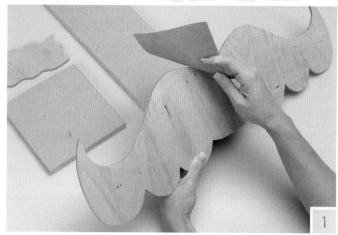

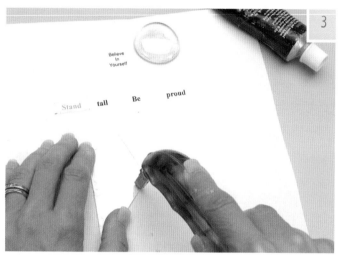

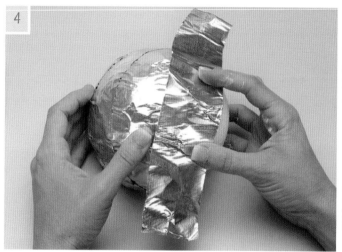

1 Prepare plywood and MDF panels

Transfer the patterns from page 121 for the wings, scroll and roof onto the plywood panels. Using a jigsaw or scroll saw, cut the plywood panels (see Using a Jigsaw, page 17). Sand all of the cut edges. Prepare the surface of each of the plywood and MDF panels with a 1:4 solution of craft glue and water.

2 Create clay tiles

Transfer the patterns for the eye, key and keyhole from page 121 onto a piece of paper and cut them out (see Transferring a Pattern, page 17). Roll the low-fire white clay to ¼" (6mm), lay the paper templates on the clay, and use the craft knife to cut out the pieces of clay. Let the clay pieces dry until they are leather hard, then smooth out any rough edges with a wet sponge. After the pieces are bone dry, apply underglaze to each piece in the following colors: white, blue and black on the eye, brown on the key and keyhole. Fire all of the tiles following the manufacturer's instructions. After the tiles have cooled, apply a clear glaze to each tile. Fire the pieces again following the manufacturer's instructions. After this firing, the clay tiles will be shiny and nonporous (see Creating Clay Tiles, page 16).

3 Create word tiles

Use your computer's word processor to type and print out the phrases "Believe In Yourself" and "Stand tall Be proud" in the font of your choice. Leave spaces between the words "Stand tall Be proud." Using a small amount of silicone adhesive, glue the flat-backed glass marble over "Believe In Yourself." Lay the clear glass over the word "Stand," score the glass around the word, and break the glass with the running pliers (see Creating Glass Tesserae, page 15). Glue the glass over the text. Repeat for each word. Cut the paper around the glass marble and clear glass rectangles.

4 Prepare dome

Use a craft knife to cut the polystyrene foam ball in half. Cover the curved side of one of the pieces with aluminum tape, forming a smooth surface for adhering tiles.

5 Complete mosaic dome

Attach the "Believe In Yourself" marble to the center of the taped dome using tile adhesive. Use wheeled tile nippers to break up the yellow stained glass. Cover the dome with yellow glass tesserae.

Allow the tile adhesive to dry completely, then grout the piece with black grout. Clean the tiles once the grout has set. Once the surface is smooth, buff the tesserae with a clean towel (see Using Grout, page 18).

Allow the grout to dry completely. Use tile adhesive to adhere the tiled dome mosaic 3" (8cm) from the top of the 36" × 5" (91cm × 13cm) MDF panel.

6 Create mosaic heart

Attach each word tile of "Stand tall Be proud" to the center of the plastic heart. Use wheeled tile nippers to break up the turquoise and lavender stained glass. Cover the area of the heart around the word tiles with purple glass tesserae and the remainder of the heart with blue glass tesserae.

Adhere the tiled heart to the 6" × 6" (15cm × 15cm) MDF panel. Use wheeled tile nippers to cut 10 1" (3cm) triangles of red stained glass. Glue these around the heart. Fill in the rest of the square using white stained-glass tesserae.

Allow the tile adhesive to dry completely. Tape the sides of the MDF panel with painter's tape, then grout the piece with black grout. Clean the tiles once the grout has set. Once the surface is smooth, buff with a clean towel.

7 Continue adding tiles

Begin adhering tiles to the 36" × 5" (91cm × 13cm) MDF panel. Mark off the bottom 3" (8cm) of the panel and outline the area with a ½" (1cm) border of yellow stained-glass tesserae. Use wheeled tile nippers to break up the mirror and fill the remainder of the area with mirror tesserae. Tape the sides of the panel and the area of the panel above the tiles with painter's tape. Mix lavender paint with white grout and grout the tiled area. Clean the tiles once the grout has set. Once the surface is smooth, buff the tesserae with a clean towel.

8 Finish tiling main panel

Use tile adhesive to adhere the clay keyhole to the 36" × 5" (91cm × 13cm) MDF panel, 7" (18cm) from the bottom edge. Use wheeled tile nippers to break the black ceramic tile into tesserae. Cover the area around and inside the keyhole with black tesserae. Attach the clay key above the yellow tiled dome. Cover the area around the key and dome with black tesserae.

Glue the clay eye 2½" (6cm) below the yellow tiled dome. Cut a black ceramic tile into ¼" (6mm) strips. Glue 1½" × ¼" (4cm × 6mm) strips above and below the clay eye. Glue 2¼" × ¼" (6cm × 6mm) strips at each corner of the eye. Glue ¾" × ¼" (2cm × 6mm) strips to each side of the eye. Use wheeled tile nippers to break the red ceramic tile into tesserae. Cover the area around the clay eye with red tesserae.

Allow the tile adhesive to dry completely. Tape around each tiled area with painter's tape, then grout the piece with white grout. Clean the tiles once the grout has set. Once the surface is smooth, buff with a clean towel.

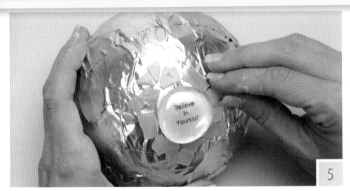

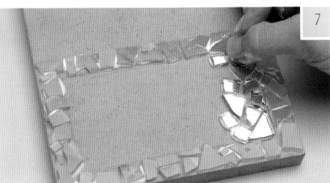

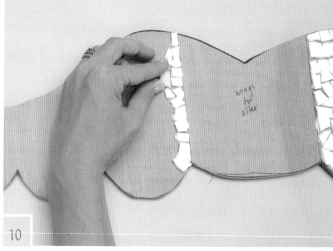

9 10

11 12

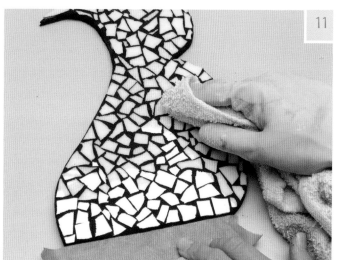

9 Paint board

Allow all of the grouted areas to dry completely. Remove the painter's tape and paint the edges of the MDF panel with black acrylic paint. Paint above the lavender grouted area and below the tiled area with the clay keyhole with white acrylic paint. Allow the paint to dry, then paint black dots on top of the white paint.

Use gold leaf paint above the tiled area with the clay keyhole area and below the tiled area with the clay eye. Allow the paint to dry, then paint black stripes over the gold. Allow all of the painted areas to dry.

10 Create mosaic wings

Using wheeled tile nippers, cut the iridescent white glass into tesserae. Cover the plywood wings in iridescent tesserae, leaving a 5" (13cm) section in the middle free of tiles. Allow the tile adhesive to dry completely.

11 Grout wings

Cover the untiled area of the wings with painter's tape, then grout the piece with black grout. Clean the tiles when the grout has set. Once the surface is smooth, buff with a clean towel.

12 Paint scroll

Paint the plywood scroll with black acrylic paint. Allow the paint to dry completely. Paint "Reach for the Stars" in white acrylic paint on the scroll, then paint white dots around the edges of the scroll. Paint several stars on the scroll with gold leaf paint. Allow the paint to dry completely.

13

13 Assemble elements

Using clear permanent glue, attach the "Reach for the Stars" scroll above the lavender grouted portion of the mosaic. Adhere the 6" × 6" (15cm × 15cm) MDF panel with the heart above the clay keyhole portion of the mosaic. Glue the iridescent wings onto the back of the 36" × 5" (91cm × 13cm) MDF panel behind the clay eye portion of the mosaic. Allow the glue to dry completely.

14 Create mosaic roof

Cover the roof piece of plywood with purple smalti. This portion of the mosaic is not grouted, so don't leave room for grout. Glue the tesserae as close together as possible. If there are gaps between the tesserae, cut tiny pieces of the smalti and fill in the gaps. Allow the tile adhesive to dry completely.

15 Prepare for hanging

Attach 2 screw eyes to the back of the piece, 4" (10cm) in from the top edge and ½" (1cm) in from the sides. Add wire to hang (see Preparing a Mosaic for Hanging, page 19).

16 Attach roof

Using clear permanent glue, attach the tiled roof to the top of the 36" × 5" (91cm × 13cm) MDF panel. Keep the mosaic upright while the glue dries.

14

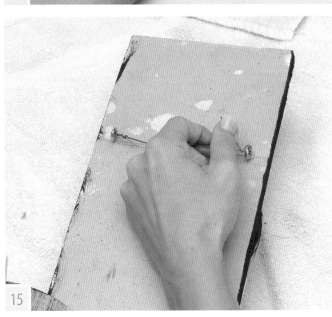

15

16

Stained Glass
Expressions

STAINED GLASS IS A BEAUTIFUL ART FORM THAT I greatly admire. Stained-glass windows are traditionally composed of pieces of glass held together in a pattern by soldered lead canes. After I had been working in mosaics for a while, I realized that stained glass could be used as mosaic tesserae. Stained glass has many qualities that make it a wonderful addition to any mosaic. First, it is produced in a wide array of unbelievable colors that are comparable only to vitreous glass, but stained glass is less expensive. You can also buy stained glass in large pieces that can be cut to any size and shape you desire, whereas vitreous glass is made in tiny squares.

I use stained glass in my mosaics in two different ways. Stained glass can be used like traditional mosaic tesserae—glued down on wood and grouted, just like the *Mystical Mandala* on page 48. A second way to include stained glass in a mosaic is to take advantage of its transparency. To do this, the pieces of glass are glued to a transparent glass base and sealed with epoxy resin instead of grout. *Celebrating Survivors* on page 44 is an example of this use of stained glass.

Tempered glass can be another unique and interesting addition to a mosaic. Also known as safety glass, tempered glass has been treated so that it will not produce sharp edges when broken. Because of the unusual way tempered glass breaks, thick pieces often contain webs of internal fractures, producing beautiful refractions within the glass. Gluing shattered tempered glass on top of an image as part of a mosaic, like I did in *Dreams of Degas* on page 52, creates a one-of-a-kind appearance.

Please be extremely careful when working with glass; protect your hands and eyes while you work. I also suggest covering your work area with disposable drop cloths for quick cleanup after working with glass so that no shards are left behind.

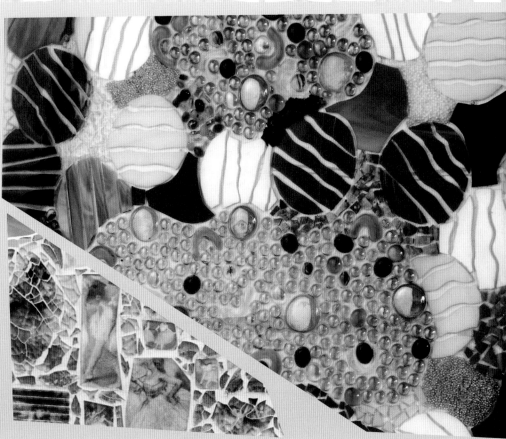

"People are like stained-glass windows. They sparkle and shine when the sun is out, but when the darkness sets in, their true beauty is revealed only if there is a light from within."

– Elizabeth Kubler-Ross

Celebrating Survivors

WE ALL GO THROUGH STRUGGLES IN OUR LIVES; some are small, but, unfortunately, some are more significant. A few of my friends and family members have gone through the difficult struggle of ovarian cancer or breast cancer. I am very happy to say that they are all survivors, and have all taught me so much about strength and perseverance.

This project was made in celebration of all who have survived breast cancer, represented by the pink ribbon. The color palette can be easily changed, however, to symbolize a different kind of struggle. This stained-glass mosaic is created on a glass base and covered with resin instead of grout, so that the beautiful effects of the stained glass shine through.

With this piece, I'd especially like to honor my friend Renee Bulosky, who fought a courageous seven-year battle with breast cancer, and who truly epitomized the meaning of strength.

Materials

Pattern (page 123)

8" × 10" (20cm × 25cm) clear glass oval

Stained glass in the following colors: iridescent white, dark pink, light pink, dark purple and light purple

Mixed-media elements such as buttons, rhinestones, charms and beads

27" (69cm) length of faux pearl trim

Seed beads in shades of pink and purple

Wheeled tile nippers

Hot glue gun and glue sticks

Clear permanent glue

Two-part epoxy resin

Embossing heat tool

Disposable cups

Craft sticks

Self-adhesive vinyl film

Wax paper

"I have heard there are troubles of more than one kind.
Some come from ahead and some come from behind.
But I've bought a big bat. I'm all ready you see.
Now my troubles are going to have troubles with me!"

– Dr. Seuss

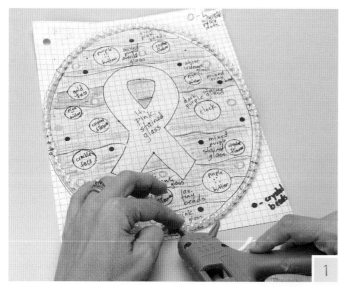
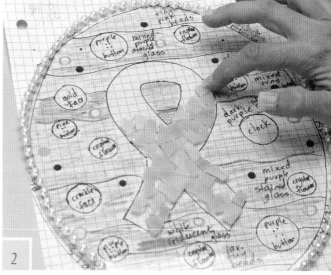
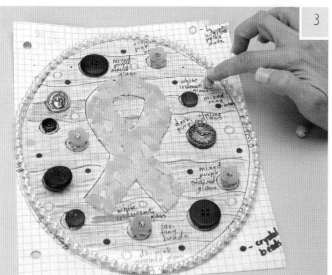
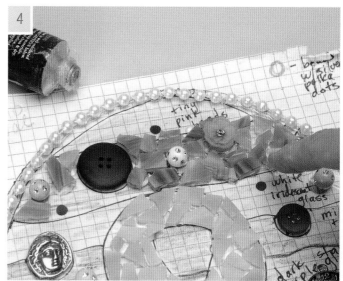

1 Begin mosaic

Make a copy of the pattern on page 123. Color code the pattern to use as a guide as you work. Lay the glass oval on top of the pattern. Use the hot glue gun to attach the faux pearl trim around the edge of the glass oval.

2 Add tesserae

Using the wheeled tile nippers, trim the light pink stained glass into small tiles. Fill in the ribbon area of the pattern with the light pink glass tiles. Use clear permanent glue to adhere the tiles to the glass oval.

3 Adhere background elements

Place the mixed-media elements in the background, planning the area around the ribbon. Cut the iridescent white, dark pink, dark purple and light purple stained glass into small tiles for the background.

4 Continue mosaic

Following the pattern, fill in the background with iridescent white, dark pink, dark purple and light purple stained-glass tiles.

◎ Wild Idea

This project calls for a plate stand, but it would also be beautiful hung in a window. Use a drill bit that is made for glass to drill through the finished piece, then attach hardware to the piece for hanging.

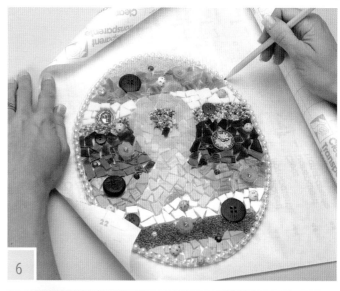
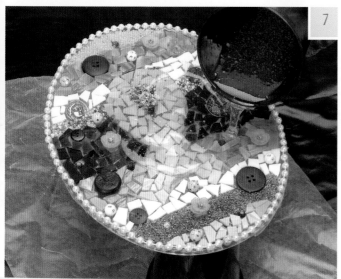
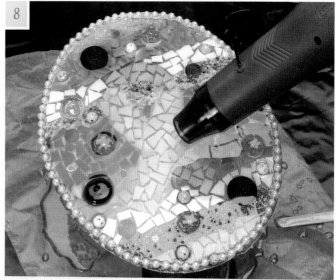

5 Add seed beads

Coat the bead portions of the glass oval with clear permanent glue. Pour seed beads onto the glue. Allow the glue to dry completely. Tap off any excess seed beads.

6 Prepare piece for epoxy

To protect the back of the project from excess drips of epoxy, cover it with a piece of self-adhesive vinyl film. Lay down a layer of wax paper shiny side up to protect your work surface. Place the project on disposable cups over the wax paper. Mix the two-part epoxy resin following the manufacturer's instructions (see Using a Two-Part Epoxy Resin, pages 20–21).

7 Pour epoxy resin

Pour the epoxy resin over the surface of the project. Start in the center and work toward the edge in a circular pattern. Spread the epoxy resin with a craft stick to cover the entire surface of the piece in an even layer. Work from the center outward, allowing any excess coating to run off the edges of the piece. Scrape the edges with a craft stick to eliminate any drips.

8 Pop air bubbles

Allow the epoxy resin to set up for about 10 minutes. As the air bubbles rise to the surface, get rid of them by passing an embossing heat tool over the surface. The carbon dioxide in the air blown by the embossing heat tool will pop the bubbles. Keep the tip of the embossing tool at least 3" (8cm) from the surface of the piece and keep it in motion.

Allow the epoxy to completely cure, following the manufacturer's guidelines. After the epoxy has cured, remove the protective backing from the piece.

Mystical Mandala

Materials

Pattern (page 120)

23" × 23" (58cm × 58cm) plywood panel

Stained glass in the following colors: dark red, light red, yellow, orange and white

Tracing vellum or white text-weight paper

White craft glue

White spray paint

Pencil

Carbon transfer paper

Glue stick

Tile adhesive

Black grout

Painter's tape

Black acrylic paint

Brown paper backing

Hot glue gun and glue sticks

Jigsaw or scroll saw

Sandpaper

Scissors

Access to a ring blade saw or glass scorer with running pliers

Lazy Susan

Towel

ONE OF THE MANY MEANINGS FOR THE SANSKRIT word *mandala* is *circle*. A mandala is a work of art that is usually circular and is used to represent many things, including wholeness, the universe and life itself. Mandala art is included in a wide variety of spiritual and religious traditions for several different purposes, including self-expression, healing and meditation.

For several spiritual and religious traditions, creating a mandala is a spiritual act. I created this pattern for myself, and you can use the pattern I've provided or design your own mandala infused with personal meaning. (You can also find a wide selection of mandala templates online or in books dedicated to the craft.) Once you have completed the mosaic, you can add another unique aspect to this project: Mount the mosaic on a lazy Susan so that it can be spun, making the final piece mystical and soothing.

"When you at last give your life—bringing into alignment your beliefs and the way you live—then, and only then, can you begin to find inner peace."

– Peace Pilgrim

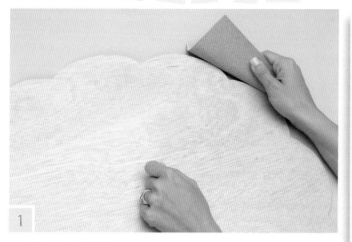

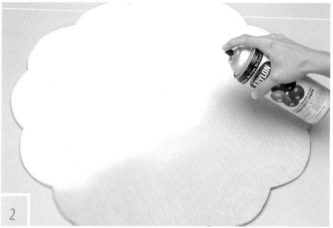

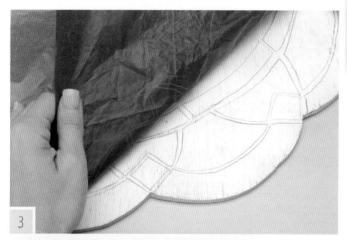

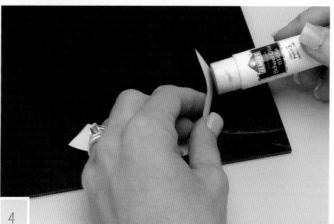

1 Prepare surface

Transfer the outside line of the mandala pattern onto the plywood panel. Use a jigsaw or scroll saw to cut the plywood (see Using a Jigsaw, page 17). Sand the cut edges, and then prepare the surface of the board with a 1:4 solution of craft glue and water.

2 Paint plywood

Allow the glue solution to dry completely. Paint one side of the board with white spray paint.

3 Transfer pattern

Let the spray paint dry, then transfer the pattern from page 120 onto the plywood. Color code the board to create a guide for placing the stained-glass tesserae.

4 Prepare glass

Copy the mandala pattern onto tracing vellum or white text-weight paper. Color code each section of the paper pattern. Cut the paper pattern into pieces. Using a glue stick, adhere the paper pieces to the corresponding colors of stained glass.

◎ Wild Idea

I keep a large disposable plastic container with a lid on my work table. When I have small pieces of glass that cannot be reused, I put them in the container. That way, when I throw away the scraps, no one will be cut by tiny shards.

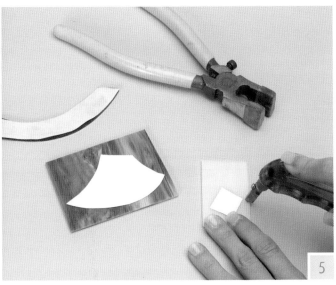

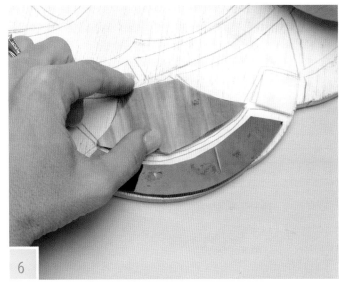

5 Cut glass

Cut out all of the stained-glass tesserae using a glass scorer and running pliers (see Creating Glass Tesserae, page 15). If you have access to a ring blade saw, it can be used to cut the glass pieces more evenly. If you use a ring blade saw for cutting the glass, carefully read and follow the manufacturer's instructions and safety information.

6 Adhere tesserae to base

Remove the paper from the glass tesserae. Clean any glue residue off of the glass pieces. Before gluing down the tesserae, arrange them on the pattern to make sure the pieces fit together with room for the grout lines. Trim the tesserae as needed. Following the mandala pattern, adhere the tesserae to the plywood with tile adhesive. Leave spaces between the tesserae for grout.

7 Grout piece

Allow the tile adhesive to dry completely. Cover the edges of the mosaic with painter's tape. Grout the piece using black grout. Let the grout set, then clean the excess grout off of the tiles (see Using Grout, page 18). Once the surface is smooth, buff the tesserae with a clean towel. Allow the grout to dry completely.

8 Mount mandala

Remove the painter's tape from the edges of the mandala. Paint the edges with black acrylic paint. Allow the paint to dry completely. Cover the back of the mosaic with brown paper backing. Mount the mandala on the lazy Susan with tile adhesive.

Dreams of Degas

I GREW UP IN THE WORLD OF DANCE: SWIRLING tutus, bright colors, long hours of classes and rehearsals, sore muscles, the exhilaration and excitement of performance. Degas's interpretation of the ballet world has always inspired me.

This project focuses on the feeling that Degas's paintings exude. The background is shaped like a tutu, and the use of the tempered glass and gold stained glass provides a glittery, reflective look. Used bookstores are a good place to find small reproductions of Degas ballerinas. You won't feel guilty cutting into a book if it cost you only a couple of dollars. This project would be wonderful for an aspiring ballerina, and you could easily customize it to fit her bedroom décor.

"A painting requires a little mystery, some vagueness, some fantasy. When you always make your meaning perfectly plain you end up boring people."

— Edgar Degas

Materials

Pattern (page 125)

24" × 24" (61cm × 61cm) plywood panel

Assorted images cut from postcards, prints and books of the ballerinas depicted in paintings by Edgar Degas

Acrylic paints in pink and purple

Clear stained glass in the following textures: hammered, quarter reeded, seeded and antique

Gold metallic stained glass

Clear tempered glass

Glue stick

White craft glue

Tile adhesive

White grout

Painter's tape

Carbon transfer paper

Pencil

Jigsaw or scroll saw

Sandpaper

Glass scorer

Running pliers

Scissors

Paintbrush

2 screw eyes

13" (33cm) length of 20-gauge steel galvanized wire

Hammer

Towel

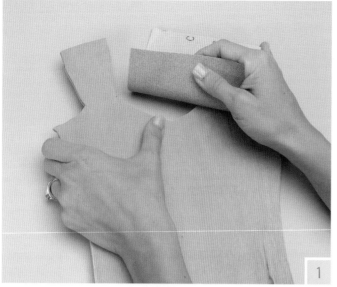

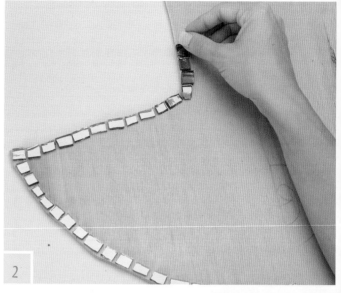

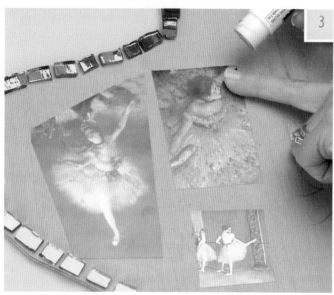

1 Prepare surface

Transfer the pattern on page 125 onto the plywood panel. Use a jigsaw or scroll saw to cut the plywood (see Using a Jigsaw, page 17). Sand the cut edges, and then prepare the surface of the MDF board with a 1:4 solution of craft glue and water.

2 Create border

Using a glass scorer and running pliers, cut the gold metallic stained glass into tesserae that are approximately ¼" × ½" (6mm × 1cm) (see Creating Glass Tesserae, page 15). Use tile adhesive to adhere the gold metallic tesserae around the edge of the plywood base.

3 Add images

Trim the ballerina images into various sizes and shapes. Using a glue stick, adhere the images to the plywood base inside the gold border.

4 Paint base

Paint around the ballerina images with pink and purple acrylic paint. Fill in any areas of the plywood base not covered by the images. Allow the acrylic paint to dry completely.

Under the Blue

THE OCEAN IS VERY IMPORTANT TO ME. I AM A fourth-generation Floridian, and I grew up going to the beach on a regular basis. My husband is an avid surfer, and goes to the beach as often as he can. We spend our summers there, and our children love the ocean as well.

The ocean has always been a symbol of life: As water, it echoes the pulse of our blood and the salt of our tears. The sound of the ocean's waves breaking onto the shore is all at once soothing and over-whelming. Nature is strong, and the ocean's cycles are never-ending.

I wanted to do an abstract version of the sea, and this project is it. I used stained glass in as many shades of blue as I could find to represent the color of water. I also designed this project not to be grouted, but to be covered with epoxy resin. I didn't want the beauty of the colored glass to compete with a grout. The epoxy resin also gives the finished piece a beautiful sheen, like calm waters.

"The ocean is a central image. It is the symbolism of a great journey."

— Enya

Materials

Pattern (page 119)

24" × 30" × ⅛" (61cm × 76cm × 3mm) glass panel

24½" × 30½" (62cm x 77cm) MDF panel

Large flat-back marbles in various shades of blue and clear

Medium flat-back marbles in various shades of blue and clear

Small flat-back marbles in various shades of blue and clear

Glass star embellishments

Glass squiggle embellishments

Stained glass in the following colors: iridescent white, iridescent black, light blue, dark blue, medium blue, turquoise and clear

Seed beads in white, silver and iridescent black

Assortment of blue beads

Carbon transfer paper

Tracing vellum or white text-weight paper

Glue stick

Clear permanent glue

White spray paint

Two-part epoxy resin

Pencil

Black permanent marker

Scissors

Access to a ring blade saw or glass scorer with running pliers

Wheeled tile nippers

Plastic trash bags

Craft sticks

Disposable cups

Embossing heat tool

Brown paper backing

Hot glue gun and glue sticks

2 screw eyes

30" (76cm) length of 20-gauge steel galvanized wire

Hammer

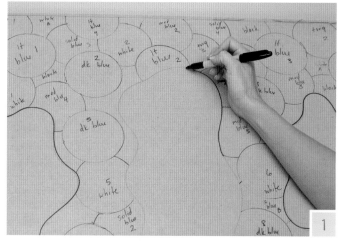

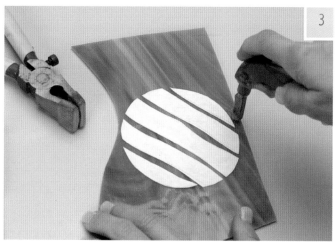
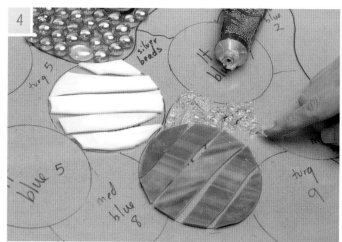

1 Prepare pattern

Transfer the pattern on page 119 to the MDF panel with carbon paper. Go over the lines with a permanent marker and color code the board to make it easier to see as you work.

2 Attach marbles

Use clear permanent glue to randomly adhere the glass star embellishments, squiggle embellishments, and the large, medium and small flat-back marbles to the glass panel inside the three "marble" areas of the pattern.

3 Cut glass

Copy the pattern on page 119 onto tracing vellum or white text-weight paper. Color code each section of the paper pattern. Cut the paper pattern into pieces. Discard the portions of the pattern that will not be covered in stained glass. Leave some of the pattern pieces for stained glass whole and cut some into squiggles. Using a glue stick, adhere the paper pieces to the corresponding colors of stained glass. Cut out all of the stained-glass tesserae using a glass scorer and running pliers (see Creating Glass Tesserae, page 15). If you have access to a ring blade saw, it can be used to cut the glass pieces more evenly. If you use a ring blade saw to cut the glass, carefully read and follow the manufacturer's instructions and safety information.

4 Adhere glass tesserae

Remove the paper from the glass tesserae. Clean any glue residue off of the glass pieces. Apply clear permanent glue to the back of the glass pieces, then adhere them to the glass panel following the pattern.

Using wheeled tile nippers, cut small glass tesserae from the remaining stained glass. Glue the small glass tesserae to the glass panel following the pattern.

⊚ Wild Idea

A nice variation on this piece would be a warm set of colors, like fire, with reds, oranges and yellows.

5 Adhere beads

Coat the bead sections of the pattern with clear permanent glue. Pour the beads onto the glue, filling the entire area. Allow the adhesive to dry, then brush off any loose beads.

6 Paint wood

Paint the top and edges of the MDF panel with white spray paint. Allow the paint to dry completely. Cover the back of the MDF panel with brown paper backing. Attach 2 eye screws to the back of the piece, 7" (18cm) in from the top edge and 2½" (6cm) in from the sides. Add wire to hang (see Preparing a Mosaic for Hanging, page 19).

7 Assemble piece

Apply five lines of clear permanent glue to the painted wood surface. Place the glass panel on top of the wood, making sure that the glass is centered on the wood. Gently press the glass down onto the wood. Allow the glue to dry completely.

8 Epoxy surface

Protect your work area with ▮▮tic trash bags. Elevate the piece above the work surface ▮▮▮ everal disposable cups. Mix the two-part epoxy resin fo▮▮▮▮g the manufacturer's instructions (see Using a Two-Part ▮▮▮ Resin, pages 20–21).

Pour the epoxy over the surface▮▮▮ project, starting in the center. Spread the epoxy to cover▮▮▮re surface of the piece in an even layer, allowing any exc▮▮▮g to run off the edges of the piece. Scrape the edges▮▮▮ft stick to eliminate any drips.

Eliminate bubbles in the epoxy with an ▮▮▮▮ heat tool. Allow the epoxy to completely cure, foll▮▮▮▮man-ufacturer's guidelines.

I BELIEVE IT IS IMPERATIVE THAT WE ALL SPEND TIME each and every day outside. Being outside gets us off the couch, off the computer and off the phone. It gives us a chance to breathe in some fresh air, feel the grass between our toes or reflect on how the sun hits the snow. No matter where we live, or what season it is, it is always important to commune with nature.

Making mosaics outside provides two great opportunities: to work in inspiring natural surroundings, and to work in natural light. Mosaics are an earthy, friendly medium. They add lots of color, originality and vibrancy to your outdoor settings, and enhance the changing seasons. Mosaics can be applied to a variety of outdoor surfaces in and around areas, including play areas, bench tops, birdbaths,

stepping-stones and walls. I used the *Welcoming Mat* on page 66 to cheer up my front porch, and laid down some *Bricks of Gold*, found on page 70, around my home as well.

When making mosaics that will be displayed outdoors, take special precautions because the weather can affect your projects. There is nothing worse than spending a lot of time working on a large project (especially an installation) and having it ruined by poor materials. Make sure to take special care sealing all of your base foundations, to use the appropriate adhesives and, after the grout cures for 48 hours, to seal the mosaic with tile and grout sealer from a local building material store. These steps will ensure beautiful, long-lasting outdoor installations and inspirations!

Outdoor Inspiration

"The day, water, sun, moon, night—I do not have to purchase these things with money."

– Plautis

Beauteous Butterfly

THE BUTTERFLY IS A POWERFUL SYMBOL OF TRANSFORMATION. It starts its life as a caterpillar and metamorphoses into a beautiful butterfly. These creatures are symbols of change, joy and color, and they provide a sense of happiness amidst impermanence. There is also something about butterflies that has a calming effect on many people.

This is a nice project to make as a gift or for yourself, to beautify a garden and welcome in guests of both the human and butterfly varieties. Although this mosaic was designed to be displayed outside, it would be lovely hung inside as well. Making a few of these butterflies in different colors and sizes and hanging them together also makes a pretty display.

Decorating a terra cotta pot—or even a whole set of them—is a great way to expand on this project. It adds even more varied whimsy to a display of natural plant life.

Materials

Pattern (page 119)

10" × 17" (25cm × 43cm) plywood panel

2 clear flat-back marbles

4" × 4" (10cm × 10cm) black ceramic tiles

Mosaic tesserae from plates, cups, bowls, etc., in a variety of shades of green

Clay pot

White craft glue

Tile adhesive

Painter's tape

White grout

Grout sealer

Pencil

Carbon transfer paper

Black permanent marker

Paintbrush

Jigsaw or scroll saw

Sandpaper

Tile nippers

Towel

Dry cloth or sponge

2 screw eyes

17" (43cm) length of 20-gauge steel galvanized wire

Hammer

"To make a wish come true, whisper it to a butterfly. Upon these wings it will be taken to Heaven and granted. For they are the messengers of the Great Spirit."

— Native American lore

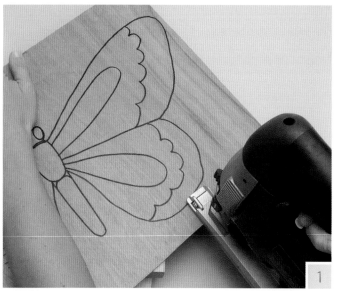

1 Cut panel

Use a black permanent marker to transfer the pattern found on page 119 to the plywood panel. Using a jigsaw or scroll saw, cut out the butterfly (see Using a Jigsaw, page 17). Sand the edges of the plywood.

2 Prepare panel

Prepare the surface of the plywood with a 1:4 solution of craft glue and water. This is particularly important on this project, as it is meant to be displayed outside and needs to be waterproof.

3 Begin mosaic

Use tile adhesive to attach clear glass marbles to the plywood board to create the butterfly's eyes. Cut the black tiles into small pieces with tile nippers. Fill in the butterfly's body with black tiles.

4 Continue adding tiles

Fill in one wing of the butterfly with the green mosaic tesserae. Fill each section with a different shade of green. Adhere tiles to the second wing, mirroring the color placement of the first wing.

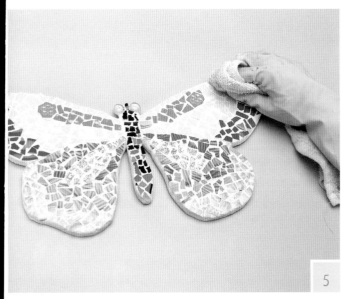

5 Grout mosaic

Once the tile adhesive is completely dry, grout the butterfly with white grout. Spread a thin layer of grout along the edges of the piece. Allow the grout to set and clean the excess grout off of the tiles (see Using Grout, page 18). Once the surface is smooth, buff the tesserae with a clean towel. Allow the grout to dry completely.

6 Weatherproof the mosaic

Apply grout sealer over the entire surface of the mosaic to weatherproof it. Make sure to seal the edges of the piece as well as the front. Allow the sealer to dry for 20 minutes, then buff the tiles clean with a dry cloth or sponge.

7 Prepare butterfly for hanging

Screw one screw eye into the top of each wing. Attach wire to the screws for hanging (see Preparing a Mosaic for Hanging, page 19).

8 Decorate clay pot to match butterfly

Mark the lip of the clay pot at 2" (5cm) intervals. Fill each 2" (5cm) square with a different shade of green mosaic tesserae. Allow the tile adhesive to dry completely. Tape off the untiled portions of the clay pot with painter's tape. Grout the tiled edge of the pot with white grout. Clean the tiles once the grout has dried. Apply grout sealer over the tiled area to weatherproof it. Allow the sealer to dry for 20 minutes, then buff the tiles clean with a dry cloth or sponge.

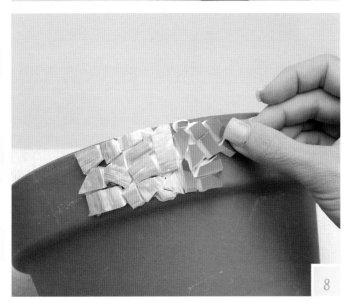

Welcoming Mat

Materials

17" × 25" (43cm × 64cm) MDF panel

21" × 29" (53cm × 74cm) piece of fiberglass mesh

Ceramic tiles in the following colors: white, blue, red, purple and dark green

12" × 12" (30cm × 30cm) slate tiles

Gray grout

Cement-based adhesive

Masking tape

Pencil

White chalk

Black permanent marker

Carbon transfer paper

Plastic wrap

Tile nippers

Tile adhesive

Scissors

Trowel

Wet tile saw, if needed

Grout sealer

Towel

During the last few years, do-it-yourself home improvement projects have soared in popularity. Many people have started taking steps to beautify the inside and outside of their homes with their own creativity and hard work. I think the trend began as a way to save money while raising the value of a home, but more and more I think people do it because they enjoy it.

Tiling a cement walkway to your house is a great way to add sophistication to a drab and lifeless outside area. There are tons of books and Web sites that can walk you step-by-step through the process of laying the tile. In this project, I've added an original twist: a mosaic welcome mat. It adds a splash of color and a unique look to the entry of your home. You can take this project as far as your imagination allows. Choose colors that suit your decorating scheme, and take the project on from there.

"A house is made of walls and beams; a home is built with love and dreams."

– Author Unknown

1 Create pattern

Write the word "welcome" on your MDF panel. Go over the lines with a black permanent marker to make the pattern easier to see as you work.

2 Prepare work surface

The MDF panel will be used only as a guide for placing tiles, it will not be a part of the finished mosaic, so cover the panel with plastic wrap to protect the board. Secure the plastic wrap to the board with masking tape. Secure the mesh over the plastic wrap.

3 Cut tiles

Using tile nippers, cut all of the ceramic tiles into tesserae. Cut the white tile pieces into square shapes for the background. Cut a slate tile into tesserae as well. Because this is a functional mosaic that will be walked on, make sure all of the pieces are at least ½" (1cm) or larger.

4 Adhere tiles

Using tile adhesive, adhere the ceramic tesserae to the mesh following the pattern on the MDF panel. Let the finished mosaic dry overnight.

5 Trim mat

Carefully remove the mesh from the plastic wrap and MDF panel. Using scissors, trim the excess mesh around the mosaic.

6 Place mosaic

Mark the area where you intend to place the mosaic with chalk. Using a trowel, lightly coat the area with a cement-based adhesive. Lay the mosaic on top of the adhesive and press it down into the adhesive gently. If necessary, replace any pieces that came loose from the mosaic.

7 Lay slate tile

Using cement-based adhesive, adhere slate tiles over the remaining area. If necessary, cut tiles to fill in small spaces, either by hand or with a wet tile saw. (For information on how to lay tile, please see *Resources* on page 126.)

8 Grout walkway

Let the adhesive dry overnight. Grout the entire area using gray grout (see Using Grout, page 18). Clean the tiles once the grout has set. Once the surface is smooth, buff the tesserae with a clean towel. Finally, seal the complete project with a grout sealer. Wait at least 24 hours before letting anyone walk on the area.

⊙ Wild Idea

Slate tiles are available at hardware stores. If you are unfamiliar with tiles, talk to the store representative when picking them out. The slate tiles have a nice texture to them, which will prevent accidents. Don't pick slick tiles that you would use inside; rain or snow makes them very slippery.

Bricks of Gold

ON A RECENT TRIP TO NORTH CAROLINA, MY FAMILY and I had a wonderful visit to the Linville Caverns. My children were enthralled by all of the crystals. My sons spent their pocket money on polished agate slices, amethyst crystals, stalagmites and stalactites.

I wanted to do something with some of the crystals to preserve our memories in a unique way. My seven-year-old son helped me with this project, which was fun to do together and very meaningful for both of us. We decided to take a few of the polished agate slices and make mosaics for our house with them.

Once the bricks were completed, we laid them as accent pieces in a brick walkway. If you don't have a brick walkway, these small mosaics are beautiful as garden decorations, doorstops or paperweights.

Materials

4" × 8" (10cm x 20cm) brick paver

1 polished agate slice

Stained glass in the following colors: gold metallic, lime green and dark green

⅛" (3mm) thick mirror

2 green flat-back marbles

11 river rocks

Tile adhesive

Painter's tape

Beige grout

Grout sealer

Paintbrush

Glass scorer

Running pliers

Large plastic bag

Towel

Dry cloth or sponge

"A treasure to a little boy does not consist of money, gems or jewelry. He will find far greater pleasure in the wonder of a rock, pebble or stick."

— Author Unknown

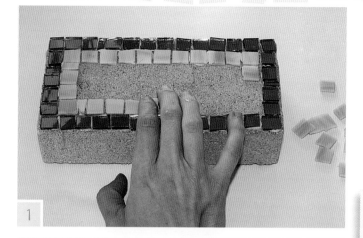

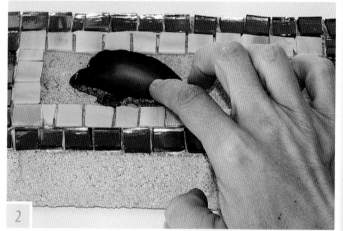

⊙ Wild Idea

Mosaics are a wonderful craft to do with children. For a safe and fun day, make sure to follow all safety precautions and supervise closely.

1 Cut tiles

Using a glass scorer and running pliers, cut the metallic gold and lime green stained glass into tesserae that are approximately ½" × ½" (1cm × 1cm) (see Creating Glass Tesserae, page 15). Using tile adhesive, glue the gold metallic tesserae around the edge of the brick to form an outer border. To form an inner border, glue the lime green tesserae along the inside edge of the gold tesserae.

2 Adhere agate slice

Randomly place the agate slice on the brick inside of the glass borders. Once you are happy with the placement, adhere it.

3 Adhere river rocks

Glue the river rocks to the brick, making a trail around the agate slice and across the brick to the edge of the border.

4 Continue adhering tiles

Using a glass scorer and running pliers, cut the ⅛" (3mm) thick mirror into tesserae. Randomly adhere a few of the pieces to the untiled portion of the brick.

5 Finish tiling

Randomly place 2 flat-backed marbles on the brick inside of the glass borders. Once you are happy with the placement, adhere them. Using a glass scorer and running pliers, cut the dark green stained glass into tesserae. Fill in the remaining untiled area with dark green stained-glass tesserae.

6 Grout mosaic

Allow the tile adhesive to dry completely. Tape the sides of the brick with painter's tape. Grout the piece using beige grout. Let the grout set, then clean the excess grout off of the tiles (see Using Grout, page 18). Once the surface is smooth, buff the tesserae with a clean towel. Remove the painter's tape and seal the brick inside a plastic bag. (Bricks are very porous, and if the grout dries too fast, the grout can crack. Allowing the brick to dry in the bag contains the humidity and prevents cracks.) Allow the grout to cure completely for 2 days.

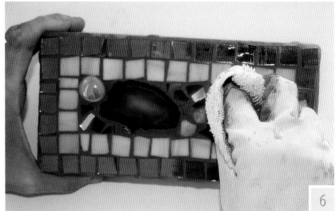

7 Seal mosaic

Apply grout sealer over the entire surface of the mosaic to weatherproof it. Make sure to seal the edges of the piece as well as the top. Allow the sealer to dry for 20 minutes, then buff the tiles clean with a dry cloth or sponge.

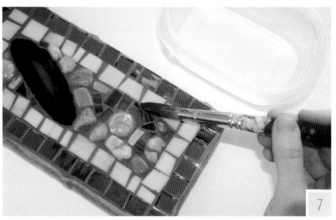

8 Lay bricks

Repeat Steps 1–7 for each mosaic brick you'd like for your patio or walkway. Lay mosaic bricks interspersed among plain bricks to create a patio or walkway. Make sure that the tops of the mosaic bricks are level with the tops of the plain bricks to prevent excess wear and tear to the mosaic bricks. If you are not familiar with laying bricks, please consult a professional to assist you.

Burst of Sunshine

WHO DOESN'T LOVE SUNSHINE? THE SUN GIVES US
energy, brings light into our lives and makes everything seem
wonderful. It is especially meaningful to see a happy and cheerful sun in the middle of a cold winter or a particularly long rainy
season. This project is a unique and interesting element to add
to a garden, pool deck or any outdoor area.

I love this project because there are so many mixed-media
elements to it. Concrete, rocks, PVC pipe, a foam swimming
noodle, stained glass, wood, paint and epoxy resin all come
together to create this cheerful piece. For a variation, try creating other shapes besides the sun, such as birds, flowers or lady-
bugs, to make a collection of mosaics.

"Keep your face to the sunshine and you cannot see the shadows."

— Helen Keller

Materials

Pattern (page 125)

10" (25cm) diameter round stepping-stone mold

8 pounds (4kg) stepping-stone concrete mix

30" (76cm) length of 1" (3cm) diameter PVC pipe

Small river rocks

2¼" (6cm) diameter foam pool noodle with 1" (3cm) diameter opening

Stained glass in the following colors: red, orange, yellow, metallic gold and turquoise

Acrylic paints in the following colors: red, orange, yellow, blue, light pink, hot pink and white

18" × 18" (46cm × 46cm) plywood panel

White grout

Grout sealer

White craft glue

Two-part epoxy resin

Tile adhesive

Black permanent marker

Plastic wrap

Craft sticks

Assortment of paint brushes

Disposable cups

Plastic trash bags

Wheeled nippers

Jigsaw or scroll saw

Sandpaper

Craft knife

Aluminum tape

Pencil

Carbon transfer paper

Embossing heat tool

2 screw eyes

18" (46cm) length of 22-gauge steel galvanized wire

Towel

Dry cloth or sponge

Hammer

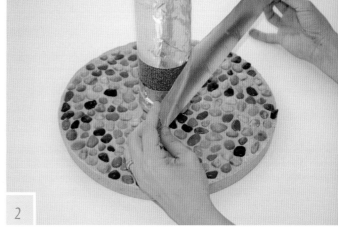

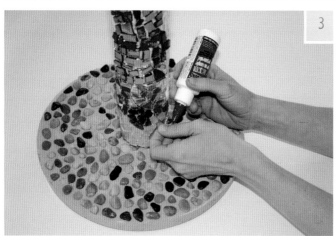

1 Create base

Following the manufacturer's instructions, mix the stepping-stone cement and pour it into the mold. Allow the cement to set up for 5–10 minutes, then push the PVC pipe into the center of the mold. While the concrete is wet, gently push small river rocks into the surface of the cement. Leave at least 1" (3cm) of the cement around the PVC pipe clear of river rocks. Let the cement dry for 48 hours in a safe spot with the PVC pipe supported in an upright position. When the cement is dry, pop it out of the mold. If any of your river rocks come loose, use tile adhesive to secure them back in.

2 Prepare surface

Cut the foam pool noodle to 29" (74cm) long and slide it down onto the PVC pipe until the pool noodle touches the cement base. Completely cover the foam with aluminum tape.

3 Adhere tiles

Cut the stained glass into small pieces using wheeled nippers (see Creating Glass Tesserae, page 15). Use a permanent marker to divide the pole into 3" (8cm) stripes. Randomly draw 8 circles over the length of the pole. Glue turquoise glass tesserae inside of the circles. Fill in the stripes with red, orange, yellow and gold glass. Allow the tile adhesive to dry overnight.

4 Grout mosaic

Cut a 12" × 12" (30cm × 30cm) square of plastic wrap. Cut a small slit in the center of the plastic wrap, just big enough to fit around the tiled pool noodle. Slide the plastic wrap down over the noodle until it is covering the cement base.

Grout the piece using white grout. Let the grout set, then clean the excess grout off of the tiles (see Using Grout, page 18). Once the surface is smooth, buff the tesserae with a clean towel. Allow the grout to dry completely. Apply grout sealer over the entire surface of the mosaic to weatherproof it. Make sure to seal the edges of the piece as well as the front. Allow the sealer to dry for 20 minutes, then buff the tiles clean with a dry cloth or sponge. Remove the plastic wrap from the base.

5 6

7 8

5 Cut plywood

Transfer the pattern found on page 125 to the plywood panel. Using a jigsaw or scroll saw, cut out the pattern (see Using a Jigsaw, page 17). Sand the edges of the plywood.

6 Paint plywood

Prepare the surface of the plywood with a 1:4 solution of craft glue and water. This is particularly important on this project, as it is meant to be displayed outside and needs to be waterproof. Allow the solution to dry completely. Using the pattern on page 125 or your own design, paint the sun with acrylic paints. Be sure to paint the back and sides of the plywood, as well.

7 Apply epoxy resin

Allow the paint to dry completely. Cover your work area with plastic trash bags. Elevate the piece above the work surface with several disposable cups. Mix the two-part epoxy resin following the manufacturer's instructions (see Using a Two-Part Epoxy

Resin, pages 20–21). Pour the epoxy over the surface of the project, starting in the center. Spread the epoxy to cover the entire surface of the piece in an even layer, allowing any excess coating to run off the edges of the piece. Scrape the edges with a craft stick to eliminate any drips. Eliminate bubbles in the epoxy with an embossing heat tool. Allow the epoxy to completely cure, following the manufacturer's guidelines.

After the epoxy resin has cured, turn the sun over and apply epoxy resin to the back of the sun as well. This will keep the sun waterproof.

8 Prepare piece to hang

Attach screw eyes and wire to the back of the plywood for hanging (see Preparing a Mosaic for Hanging, page 19).

Indoor Installations

THEY SAY THAT HOME IS WHERE THE HEART IS. I believe that a home says a lot about its occupant. Your home could be a one-bedroom apartment or a ten-bedroom mansion; it's the environment we create that's important. Home should be a place of refuge, a place to relax and feel comfortable.

I believe that your home should reflect your personality. What colors do you like? Do you like to bring the natural world into your home? Are you into photography or art? Your home should reflect the things that you like and enjoy. Surround yourself with beauty.

One of my favorite ways to decorate my home is with artwork, both my children's and my own. This chapter focuses on four projects that are perfect for a home environment. All of them are designed to be unique, eclectic pieces that are one of a kind, just for your home. I happen to have a few small children in our home right now, so I like things to be brightly colored and kid-friendly. Because your tastes may not be the same as mine, all of these projects are easily adaptable in color, size or subject to different tastes. So go ahead, express yourself!

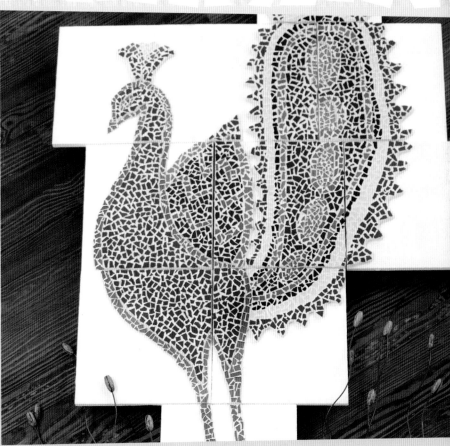

"Every spirit builds itself a house, and beyond its house a world; and beyond its world a heaven. Know then that world exists for you."

— Ralph Waldo Emerson

Proud Peacock

Materials

Pattern (page 122)

10 10" × 10" (25cm × 25cm) MDF panels

4" × 4" (10cm × 10cm) ceramic tiles in the following colors: denim blue, light blue, purple, lavender, turquoise and seafoam green

Gold metallic stained glass or gold smalti

White craft glue

White grout

White acrylic paint

Markers or colored pencils to match the tiles and glass

Pencil

Carbon transfer paper

Black permanent marker

Wheeled tile nippers

Tile adhesive

Painter's tape

Paintbrush

Brown paper backing

Hot glue gun and glue sticks

2 screw eyes

8' (2.5m) length of 20-gauge steel galvanized wire

Hammer

Damp towel or sponge

Towel

THIS LARGE-SCALE PROJECT FEATURES A VIBRANT peacock. In some societies, peacocks are symbols of beauty and richness, and in others, symbols of acceptance and openness. In Buddhism, a peacock symbolizes wisdom, and in Christianity a peacock represents immortality. I've always had an affinity for the beauty of the peacock.

I wanted to give this mosaic a unique structure, so I staggered the MDF panels. For a more even, organized look, this mosaic could be worked on one large panel, although that would be very heavy, or worked on panels arranged in a geometric grid. The beautiful colors of a peacock—greens, blues and purples, highlighted with gold—give this mosaic a deep richness. To make this piece truly royal, try painting the edges of each wooden square with gold leaf.

"The pride of the peacock is the glory of God."

– William Blake

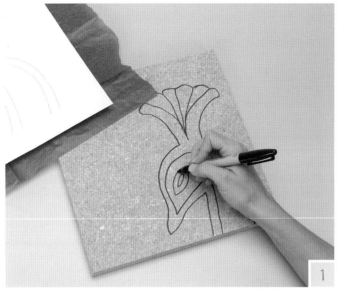

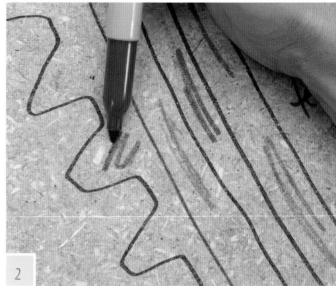

1 Prepare wood

Prepare the surface of each MDF panel with a 1:4 solution of craft glue and water. Allow the panels to dry completely. Transfer the pattern on page 122 to the MDF panels with transfer paper. Go over the carbon lines with a permanent marker to make it easier to see as you work.

2 Mark boards

To avoid confusion, color code each MDF panel with markers or colored pencils.

3 Adhere tesserae

Use wheeled tile nippers to cut the gold metallic stained glass and ceramic tiles into small pieces. Use tile adhesive to adhere the tesserae to the MDF panel following the peacock pattern. Allow the tile adhesive to dry completely.

4 Paint panels

Paint the untiled areas and edges of each MDF panel with white acrylic paint. Be careful not to get paint on the tesserae. Allow the paint to dry completely. (If paint does get on the tesserae, let it dry completely, then scrape it off.)

5 Cover painted areas

Use painter's tape to protect the painted areas of each panel bordering the tesserae. It is not necessary to cover the entire painted area with painter's tape, as the white grout will not stain the paint. If any grout does get on the uncovered painted areas, clean the grout off of the paint with a damp cloth.

6 Grout mosaic

Grout the mosaic with white grout (see Using Grout, page 18). Be sure to push the grout down in all of the spaces between the tesserae.

7 Clean tiles

Allow the grout to set (approximately 10 minutes). Clean the grout from the tiles with a damp towel or sponge. Once the surface is smooth, buff the tesserae with a clean towel.

8 Prepare panels for hanging

Cover the back of each panel with brown backing paper. Attach 2 screw eyes to the back of the piece, 2" (5cm) in from the top edge and 2" (5cm) in from the sides. Add wire to hang each individual board in position (see Preparing a Mosaic for Hanging, page 19).

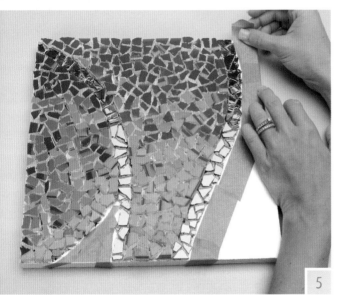

5

6

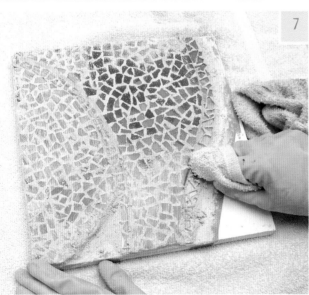

7

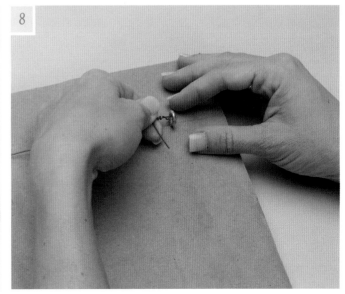

8

Functional Table

A FEW YEARS AGO, MY HUSBAND AND I BOUGHT A new kitchen table. Three children and many art projects later, we finally decided that the scratched and dented table needed to be replaced with something more respectable. Finally, I had a nice wood table to mosaic!

When you are choosing a piece of furniture to mosaic, don't choose laminated wood or anything that isn't very sturdy and strong. Remember, the base you choose needs to support a lot of weight from the tiles and grout. I just happened to have an extra table for this piece, but furniture is easy to find at garage sales and thrift stores.

Because I enjoy quilting, I based this mosaic table on a very simple patchwork pattern. A piece like this will be a unique addition to your home décor.

"Being happy doesn't mean that everything is perfect. It means that you've decided to look beyond the imperfections"

— Author unknown

Materials

36" × 48" (91cm × 122cm) tabletop or MDF panel

4" × 4" (10cm × 10cm) black ceramic tiles

Mosaic tesserae from a wide variety of ceramic tiles, plates, cups, bowls, etc.

1 pint (½ L) white latex house paint

Black permanent marker

Tile adhesive

White grout

Grout sealer

Polyurethane

Painter's tape

Tile nippers

Plastic drop cloth

Sandpaper or power sander

Tape measure

Paintbrush

Pencil

Towel

1 Prepare base

Working in a well-ventilated area, sand the tabletop with sandpaper or a power sander. Once the tabletop is smooth, clean away any saw dust. Using a tape measure and pencil, mark off a grid on the tabletop. Go over the transfer lines with black permanent marker to make the pattern easier to see as you work. Because my table measures 36" × 48" (91cm × 122cm), I decided to divide the surface into 5 5" × 5" (13cm × 13cm) squares across and 8 5" × 5" (13cm × 13cm) squares down. Divide your own tabletop as you see fit.

2 Begin adhering tiles

Cut the black ceramic tiles into 1" × 1" (3cm × 3cm) squares. Using tile adhesive, adhere the black tiles around the edge of the table and along the marked grid.

3 Cut tesserae

Cut the crockery and tiles into mosaic tesserae that are approximately ½"–1" (1cm–3cm) in size.

4 Finish adhering tesserae

Glue the mosaic tesserae into the outlined squares. Leave room between the tesserae for grout.

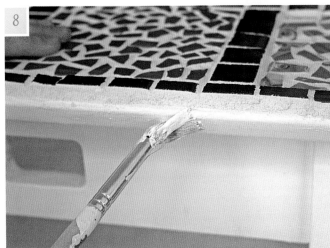

5 Paint base

Allow the tile adhesive to dry completely. Place the table on a plastic drop cloth to catch any spilled paint or grout. Paint the base and legs of the table with white latex house paint.

6 Grout mosaic

Allow the paint to dry completely. Cover the painted areas with painter's tape. Grout the mosaic with white grout. Clean the tiles once the grout has set. Once the surface is smooth, buff the tesserae with a clean towel (see Using Grout, page 18).

7 Seal mosaic

Allow the grout to dry completely. Remove the painter's tape and clean off any remaining grout. Apply a grout sealer to your mosaic. Touch up the white paint if needed.

8 Seal paint

Allow the paint and grout sealer to dry completely. Apply a coat of polyurethane to the base and legs of the table to seal the paint.

Communication Collection

Materials

12" × 24" (30cm × 61cm) MDF panel

4" × 4" (10cm × 10cm) ceramic tiles in the following colors: cobalt blue, red and white

2 ceramic cereal-themed mugs

Stained glass in the following colors: gold metallic and clear

Mosaic tesserae from a variety of handmade ceramic tiles in black, white and yellow

Assorted cereal-themed images

Orange metallic foil paper

4½" × 12" (11cm × 30cm) piece of corkboard

12" (30cm) length of beaded ribbon fringe

Clear flat-back marbles

Acrylic paint in white and tan

Thumbtacks

White craft glue

Clear permanent glue

Tile adhesive

Painter's tape

White grout

Wheeled tile nippers

Paintbrush

Hot glue gun and glue sticks

Brown paper backing

2 screw eyes

12" (30cm) length of 20-gauge steel galvanized wire

Hammer

Towel

Bubble wrap or towels

Scissors (optional)

Cereal-themed images from Icons—Krazy Kids' Food! *by Steve Roden and Dan Goodsell*

IN THIS BUSY DAY AND AGE WE ARE CONSTANTLY bombarded with messages and reminders. Soccer practice changes to a different day, the dentist calls to cancel an appointment, your best friend calls to chat while you are out. This project is a fun and clever way to keep communication open with your family by creating a central location for all of those messages. You can keep pens or pencils in one mug and scrap paper in the other for easy access. Hang the mosaic near the phone, and messages can be written down and tacked onto the corkboard.

To make this mosaic family friendly, I chose a cute retro theme with vintage cereal images. I love the colorful images, and since our central phone area is in the kitchen, the theme works well with the decor. Customize the mugs, colors and images to fit your décor and create a place to collect your own communications.

"Tell me and I'll forget; show me and I may remember; involve me and I'll understand."

– **Chinese proverb**

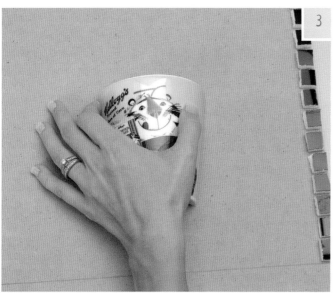

1 Create border

Prepare the MDF panel with a 1:4 solution of craft glue and water. Allow the solution to dry completely. Mark off the bottom 4½" (11cm) of the board. This area will be covered with the corkboard and should not be tiled. Using wheeled tile nippers, cut the cobalt ceramic tiles into tesserae that are approximately ½" × ½" (1cm × 1cm) (see Nipping Tile, page 14). Use tile adhesive to adhere the cobalt tesserae around the edge of the MDF panel, except for the bottom 4½" (11cm).

2 Cut mugs

To cut the mug in half, grip the mug on the side opposite the handle with the wheeled tiled nippers. Apply even pressure and squeeze until the mug breaks into two pieces. (If you'd like, practice on an extra mug before cutting your decorative mugs.)

3 Attach mugs

Attach the mug halves to the MDF board with tile adhesive. Space the mugs about 5" (13cm) apart, one above the other in the center of the MDF panel.

4 Attach decorative tesserae

Begin to fill in the background of the mosaic with the handmade ceramic tesserae, metallic gold stained glass, and the orange metallic paper and cereal images covered with clear glass.

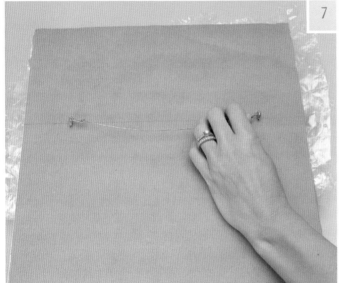

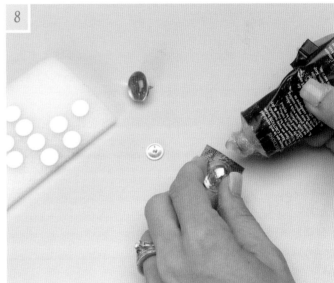

5 Complete mosaic

Fill in the remaining area of the mosaic with tesserae from the white and red ceramic tiles. Allow the tile adhesive to dry completely. Tape the sides with painter's tape. Mix tan acrylic paint and white grout to create tan grout. Grout the piece. Let the grout set, then clean the excess grout off of the tiles (see Using Grout, page 18). Once the surface is smooth, buff the tesserae with a clean towel. Allow the grout to dry completely.

6 Attach corkboard

Remove the painter's tape from the edges of the MDF panel. Paint the edges with white acrylic paint. Allow the paint to dry completely. Adhere the corkboard to the bottom of the MDF panel with a hot glue gun. Use the hot glue gun to attach the beaded ribbon fringe to the bottom of the corkboard.

7 Prepare for hanging

Cover the back of the MDF panel with brown backing paper. Whenever the mosaic is turned over, prop it up on towels or bubble wrap to support and protect the mugs on the front. Attach 2 screw eyes to the back of the piece, 5" (13cm) in from the top edge and 2" (5cm) in from the sides. Add wire to hang (see Preparing a Mosaic for Hanging, page 19).

8 Create thumbtacks (optional)

Place a dab of clear permanent glue on the back of a clear flat-back marble. Adhere the marble to a piece of orange metallic paper. Cut the paper to the size of the marble. Glue a thumbtack to the back of the metallic paper.

Capfuls of Color

THIS MOSAIC PROJECT IS FULL OF MIXED-MEDIA elements, and it is not for people who don't like color! The bottle caps are decorated with scrapbooking papers and images from magazines, then filled with epoxy resin to create a completely original mosaic element. Use this chalkboard to provide daily inspiration; try writing uplifting messages on it daily. This is also a wonderful gift for a child: It's so much fun to write on, especially since it is easy to erase and create new pictures or messages. To personalize this piece, change the color scheme—including the tesserae, mixed-media elements and paints—so that it matches your décor.

"Enthusiasm is excitement with inspiration, motivation and a pinch of creativity."

— Bo Bennett

Materials

19½" × 23" (50cm x 58cm) MDF panel

Acrylic paint in the following colors: turquoise, magenta, lime green, black and white

Chalkboard finish spray paint

Pink stained glass

Black grout

Chalk holder (tile holder from the board game Scrabble shown here)

52 bottle caps

Decorative papers (scrapbooking paper and magazine pages shown here)

24mm circle template

Mixed media elements such as buttons, rhinestones, charms and beads

White craft glue

Tile adhesive

Two-part epoxy resin

Pencil

Black permanent marker

Scissors

Plastic trash bags

Towel

Paintbrushes

Painter's tape

Wheeled tile nippers

Embossing heat tool

Disposable cups

Craft sticks

Brown packing paper

Hot glue gun and glue sticks

2 screw eyes

12" (30cm) length of 20-gauge steel galvanized wire

Hammer

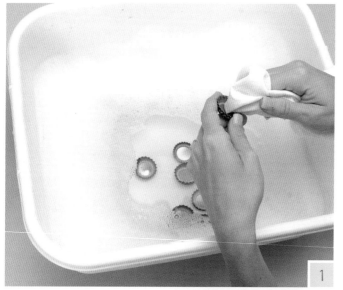

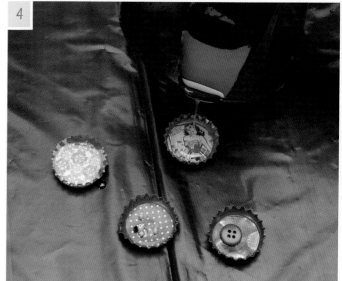

1 Clean bottle caps

Clean the bottle caps in hot, soapy water to remove any residue. Allow the bottle caps to dry completely.

2 Decorate bottle caps

Use the 24mm circle template to draw circles on various pieces of scrapbooking paper and pictures torn from magazines. Cut out the circles and glue them in the bottle caps with white craft glue. Paint a thin layer of white craft glue on top of the paper. Allow the glue to dry completely.

3 Add mixed-media elements

Adhere mixed-media elements inside several of the bottle caps with white craft glue. Vary the color combinations and decorations for a fun, eclectic look. Allow the glue to dry completely.

4 Pour epoxy resin

Protect your work area with plastic trash bags. Mix the two-part epoxy resin following the manufacturer's instructions (see Using a Two-Part Epoxy Resin, pages 20–21). Pour the epoxy resin into the bottle caps, filling them completely.

5 Finish bottle caps

Eliminate bubbles in the epoxy with an embossing heat tool. Allow the epoxy to completely cure, following the manufacturer's guidelines.

6 Prepare board

Prepare the border of the MDF board with a 1:4 solution of craft glue and water. When dry, use a black permanent marker to mark borders around the MDF panel at 1" (3cm) and 2" (5cm) in from the edge. Fill the inner 1" (3cm) border with turquoise acrylic paint. Allow the paint to dry completely.

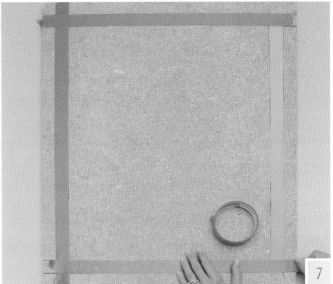

7 Cover painted areas

Cover the turquoise border completely with painter's tape.

8 Paint board

Paint the area inside of the turquoise border with chalkboard finish spray paint. Allow the paint to dry completely. To completely cover the MDF panel, use multiple coats of chalkboard paint if necessary.

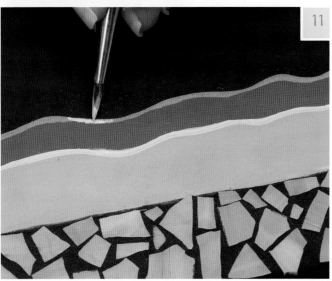

9

10

11

12

9 Tile border

Pull off the ends of painter's tape that extend into the unpainted border of the panel, but leave the turquoise border covered. Using the wheeled tile nippers, trim the pink stained glass into small tiles. Use tile adhesive to fill in the outer border of the panel with the light pink glass tiles.

10 Grout piece

Allow the tile adhesive to dry completely. Tape off the sides of the MDF panel with painter's tape, then grout the piece with black grout. Clean the tiles once the grout has set. Once the surface is smooth, buff the tesserae with a clean towel (see Using Grout, page 18).

11 Paint inner borders

Allow the grout to dry completely. Remove the painter's tape from the MDF panel. Paint a wavy magenta border over the edge of the turquoise border. Allow the paint to dry completely. Outline the magenta border with thin lines of white acrylic paint.

12 Attach bottle caps

Use white craft glue to adhere the decorated bottle caps over the magenta and turquoise border all the way around the board, leaving a 7¼" (18cm) opening at the center bottom of the board for the chalk ledge.

◎ Wild Idea

Black grout takes longer to dry than white or tan grout, and is also messier. Make sure to let black grout dry completely for a neat finished appearance.

13 Paint chalk ledge

Paint the chalk ledge with lime green acrylic paint. Allow the paint to dry completely.

14 Attach ledge

Using white craft glue, adhere the chalk ledge to the board over the open area on the turquoise border. Allow the glue to dry completely.

15 Paint edges

Paint the edges of the MDF board with black acrylic paint. Allow the paint to dry completely.

16 Prepare for hanging

Cover the back of the MDF panel with brown backing paper. Attach 2 screw eyes to the back of the piece, 5" (13cm) in from the top edge and 3" (8cm) in from the sides. Add wire to hang (see Preparing a Mosaic for Hanging, page 19).

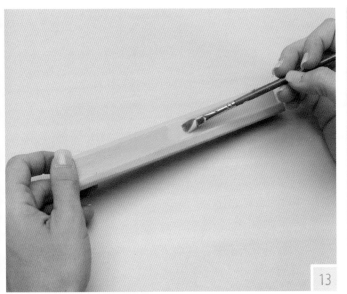

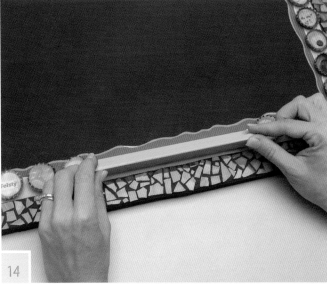

13 14

15 16

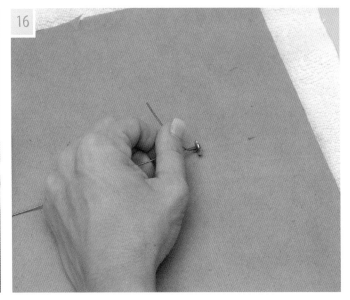

REMEMBER WHEN YOU WERE A CHILD, AND TIME SEEMED to stretch on forever? Being bored was the most painful thing that could happen to you. When you were 10 you couldn't wait to be 13, and then 16, and then 21. Then, all of sudden, you wake up, and your own children are half grown. The older we get, the faster time seems to go by, and being bored is definitely part of the past.

The projects in this chapter are meant to capture moments in time. There are many ways to capture precious memories; taking video recordings, writing special memories down in a journal, scrapbooking or taking photographs are just a few options. Making visual art is another special way to record memories. The following mosaics represent a way to capture a special moment in time.

There are different types of moments to capture as we age: what our children or other loved ones looked like at various stages in life, how we felt about different things, what was important to us. Other important things to remember are our favorite things, like books, movies, foods and travel. Capturing memories helps create a picture of who we were and how we became the people we are today. Using mosaic artwork to capture these moments in time is a very unique way to do it.

We use a large variety of materials in this chapter. From *Sugar and Spice* on page 104, which uses classic smalti, to *Snips and Snails* on page 100, which is a series of paper mosaics, this chapter is full of mixed-media mosaic ideas to help you capture special moments in time.

Moments in Time

She lived vicariously through no one.

"Realize that now, in this moment of time, you are creating. You are creating your next moment. That is what's real."

– Sara Paddison

Snips and Snails

OH, TO BE A YOUNG BOY. RUNNING AROUND CHASING the dog, catching frogs and lizards, sneaking cookies and resisting Mom's kisses. Sticking your tongue out at the girls, riding bikes around the neighborhood, playing football until the sun finally sets, reading books about adventure. Obviously I've never been a little boy, but as a mother, my sons' childhood days make me smile. They are all about living in the moment, having fun and constantly learning. I love to capture my sons in different phases of their boyhood.

This project is quick and easy, with no messy grout or cut tiles to deal with, but the effect is stunning. I particularly like to see a grouping of these mosaics, with two or more hung next to each other. This project has many adaptations. You can easily change the size or shape, and it looks wonderful for all different kinds of pictures, not just portraits. Landscapes and still-life photos make very interesting pieces, as well.

"A boy is a magical creature—you can lock him out of your workshop, but you can't lock him out of your heart."

– Allan Beck

Materials

Photograph of your choice

Decorative paper (scrapbooking paper shown here)

12" × 12" (30cm × 30cm) piece of white cardstock

12" × 12" (30cm × 30cm) piece of corrugated cardboard

12" × 12" (30cm x 30cm) scrapbooking frame

White craft glue or glue stick

Paper cutter

Ruler

Pencil

Hot glue gun and glue sticks

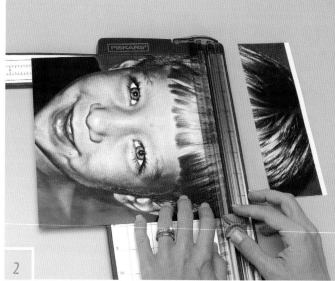

1 Prepare base

Cut the white cardstock to 10½" × 10½" (27cm × 27cm). This piece will form the base of the mosaic.

2 Enlarge photo

Select a photo for the mosaic. Take the photo to a local copy center, and have it enlarged to 8" × 10" (20cm × 25cm). Trim the picture down to 8" × 8" (20cm x 20cm) with the paper cutter.

3 Begin cutting photo

Cut the photo into 8 1" (3cm) strips. As each strip is cut, carefully lay them out in order so that the pieces don't get mixed up.

4 Finish cutting photo

Cut each of the 8 strips into 8 1" (3cm) squares. Again, make sure to lay the squares out in the correct order as they are cut.

5 Begin mosaic

Mark a 1" (3cm) border along each edge of the cardstock. Using craft glue or a glue stick, adhere the four corner squares of the photo to the cardstock inside the border. From there, glue the remaining pieces of the picture to the white cardstock. For a precise, geometric mosaic, mark a grid on the cardstock and follow it when placing the photo squares. For a more organic look, eyeball the placement of each photo square.

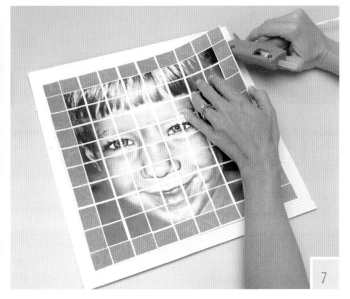

6 Add decorative paper

Using the paper cutter, cut 36 1" (3cm) squares from the decorative paper. Adhere the decorative paper squares to the border of the white cardstock. Trim the pieces of decorative paper as needed to fit inside the border.

7 Mount mosaic

Using a hot glue gun, attach the cardstock to the corrugated cardboard so that a ¾" (2cm) border of corrugated cardboard shows around the cardstock.

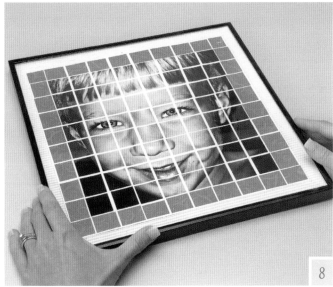

8 Frame mosaic

Secure the mosaic in the frame.

Sugar and Spice

AFTER THREE BOYS, MY HUSBAND AND I WERE THRILLED
to add to our family with the birth of our only daughter. She is such a
joy to our family, and I wanted to capture her sweet, smiling face in a
unique way.

I'll be honest with you—smalti has never been my favorite mosaic
medium. I started out doing mosaics using the most inexpensive items I
could find: usually ceramic tiles and found crockery. They have remained
my cornerstone materials. However, there are a lot of advantages to
using smalti. The colors are absolutely breathtaking and come in such
a wonderful variety. Mosaics made from smalti are rarely grouted.
Portraits are often created from smalti, so I think a portrait is a perfect
project to start with if you've never worked with smalti before.

"A daughter is a miracle that never ceases to be miraculous...
full of beauty and forever beautiful...loving and caring and
truly amazing."

— Deanna Beisser

Materials

11" × 14" (28cm × 36cm) MDF panel

Photograph

1 lb. (.5 kg) black smalti

1 lb. (.5 kg) white smalti

Carbon transfer paper

Black permanent marker

Pencil

Tile adhesive

Clear silicone adhesive

White craft glue

11" × 14" (28cm × 36cm) picture frame

Computer, scanner and printer

Photo-editing software such as Adobe
Photoshop

Wheeled tile nippers

Protective eyewear

1

1 Choose photo

Choose a photograph. If you are using a photograph of a person, I suggest using a head shot, because fine details will be lost when the design is tiled. Scan the photo and open it in a photo-editing program. If the photo is in color, change it to black and white within the photo-editing software. Next, eliminate the details from the photograph, leaving only the main elements of the image. To do this in Adobe Photoshop, choose the Sketch option, then the Stamp option from the Filter menu. Alter the Light/Dark Balance and Smoothness for high contrast with distinct lines. Print the photo at 11" x 14" (28cm x 36cm). Many computer printers don't print pages this large, so enlarge the photo on a copier if necessary.

2

2 Prepare surface

Prepare the surface of the MDF panel with a 1:4 solution of craft glue and water. Allow the panel to dry completely. Transfer the major details of the photo to the MDF panel using carbon transfer paper.

3

3 Enhance outline

Go over the transfer lines with black permanent marker to make the pattern easier to see as you work.

4 Cut smalti

Cut the smalti with wheeled tile nippers. Cut tiny pieces to outline shapes and to use in small spaces. Cut medium-size pieces to fill in large areas. Smalti is different than the other types of tesserae used in this book because it tends to break off into tiny shards that need to be disposed of properly. When cutting smalti pieces, it is very important to wear protective eyewear and to work in an enclosed area.

4

5

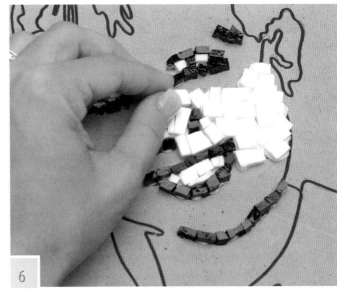

6

7

8

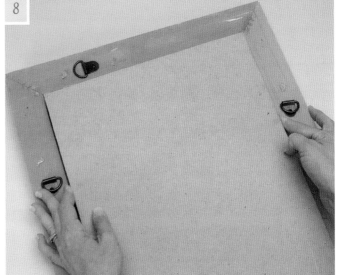

5 Begin mosaic

Begin outlining the major details of the design with tiny smalti pieces. Use the enlarged photo as a guide for color placement. This mosaic is not grouted, so don't leave room for grout. Use tile adhesive to adhere the tesserae as close together as possible. If there are gaps between the tesserae, cut tiny pieces of the smalti and fill in the gaps.

6 Continue adding tiles

Fill in the rest of the face and clothing with white smalti. Again, place the tesserae close together and fill in any gaps with tiny pieces of smalti.

7 Finish mosaic

Fill in the background of the mosaic with black smalti pieces. Allow the mosaic to dry overnight.

8 Frame

Run a line of clear silicone adhesive around the inside edge of the frame and place the mosaic lightly facedown in the opening of the frame. Allow the glue to dry overnight.

The Caged Bird Sings

Materials

Patterns (page 126)

10" × 14" (25cm × 36cm) MDF panel

21" × 48" (53cm × 122cm) MDF panel

Large assortment of decorative papers (scrapbooking papers and pages from magazines shown here)

Stained glass in the following colors: clear, black, cobalt blue, silver metallic, yellow

Image of an eye (image from a magazine shown here)

Acrylic paints in the following colors: flesh, blue, black, yellow, gray, white, green and red

Pencil

Carbon transfer paper

Black permanent marker (optional)

White craft glue

Glue stick

Clear permanent glue

Tile adhesive

Painter's tape

White grout

Jigsaw

Sandpaper

Assortment of paintbrushes

Scissors

Glass scorer

Running pliers

Wheeled tile nippers

2-4 screw eyes

1-2 12" (30cm) lengths of 20-gauge steel galvanized wire

Towel

A WELL-KNOWN POEM BY LEGENDARY AUTHOR Maya Angelou, *I Know Why the Caged Bird Sings*, inspired me to make this project. The symbolism of birds and the possibility of flight are deeply meaningful to me. In this piece, a girl is holding a cage, which represents the entrapment of a feathered being, disabling it from flying and being free. However, the bird is not in the cage; it is sitting on the girl's shoulder because she has decided to let it go. These images symbolize freedom and the possibility of flight. And by using pieces of scrapbooking papers covered by pieces of glass, I was able to include a rainbow of colors.

"... the caged bird sings of freedom."

—Maya Angelou

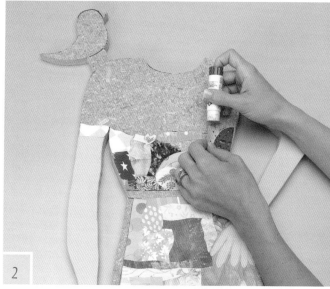

1 Prepare MDF panels

Transfer the patterns on page 126 to the MDF panels. Cut out both pieces using a jigsaw (see Using a Jigsaw, page 17). Sand the edges, then prepare the surface of each piece with a 1:4 solution of craft glue and water. When dry, draw the interior lines of the patterns on the MDF panels. If you prefer, you can go over the lines of the pattern with a black permanent marker. Paint the arms, legs and face of the girl using flesh-colored acrylic paint.

2 Fill in dress

Fill in the inside of the girl's dress using small pieces of decorative paper adhered with a glue stick. Leave a blank border around the skirt, and a blank area for the belt.

3 Paint border

Paint a belt and border around the girl's skirt using black acrylic paint. Allow the paint to dry completely, then add white dots of acrylic paint to the border and belt.

4 Trim tiles

Using wheeled tile nippers, trim the black stained glass into tiles that are approximately ½" (1cm) squares and ¼" (6mm) squares (see Creating Glass Tesserae, page 15).

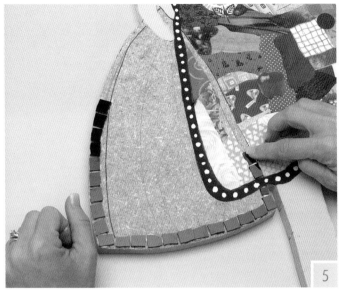

5

6

7

8

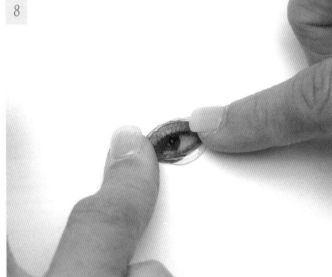

5 Finish birdcage

Outline the birdcage and its wires with ½" (1cm) black stained-glass tiles. Outline the door on the birdcage with ¼" (6mm) black stained-glass tiles. Once the tile adhesive is dry, paint the interior of the cage with white acrylic paint.

6 Tile dress

Score and break the clear ⅛" (3mm) glass into pieces of different sizes and shapes. Apply clear permanent glue to the glass pieces, then adhere them over the decorative papers and painted border of the girl's dress.

7 Create eye tile

Lay a 1½" × 1½" (4cm × 4cm) piece of clear ⅛" (3mm) glass over the eye image. Using the scoring tool, score the glass along the outline of the eye.

8 Finish eye

Break the glass along the score lines with running pliers. Adhere the glass to the eye with clear permanent glue.

9 Cover bird

Adhere the glass-covered eye image to the bird on the girl's shoulder. Outline the bird's legs with the remaining ¼" (6mm) black stained-glass tiles. Trim the cobalt blue stained glass into small tiles. Fill in the rest of the bird with cobalt blue stained-glass tiles.

10 Grout piece

Allow the tile adhesive to dry completely. Tape off the painted areas with painter's tape, then grout the piece with white grout. Clean the tiles once the grout has set. Once the surface is smooth, buff the tesserae with a clean towel (see Using Grout, page 18).

11 Paint edges

Allow the grout to dry completely. Remove the painter's tape from the painted areas. Paint all of the edges of the piece with acrylic paint (flesh for arms and legs, black for dress and cage, blue for the bird). Paint the top and edges of the bird's beak yellow. Allow the paint to dry completely.

12 Begin crown

Using the wheeled tile nippers, trim the silver metallic stained glass into small tiles. Fill in the crown on the girl's head with silver metallic tesserae.

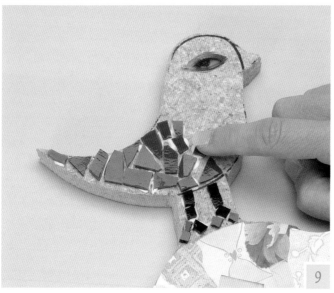
9

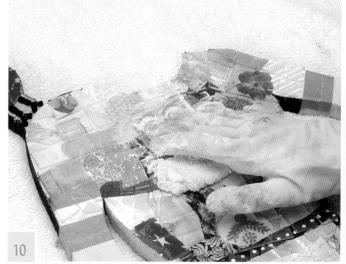
10

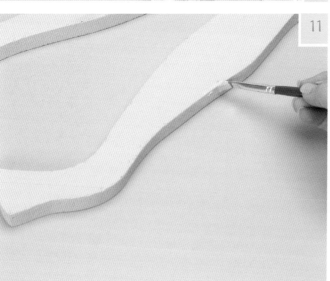
11

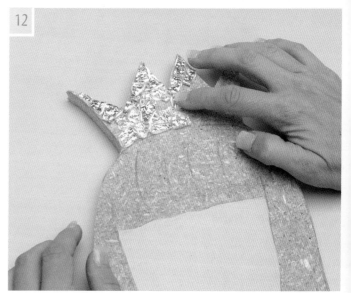
12

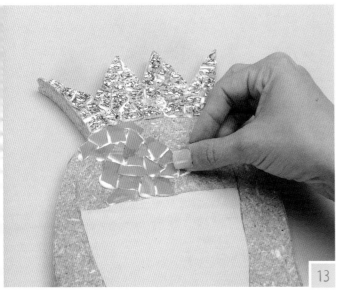

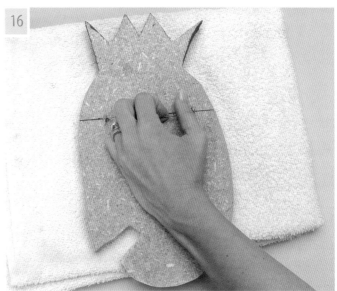

13 Add tiles for hair

Using the wheeled tile nippers, trim the yellow stained glass into small tiles. Fill in the girl's hair with yellow tesserae.

14 Grout piece

Allow the tile adhesive to dry completely. Tape off the girl's face with painter's tape. Grout the piece with white grout. Clean the tiles once the grout has set. Once the surface is smooth, buff the tesserae with a clean towel. Allow the grout to dry completely.

15 Complete face

Remove the painter's tape from the painted areas. Paint the girl's face with acrylic paints and add details with a pencil. Allow the paint to dry completely. Paint the edges of the panel with acrylic paints.

16 Prepare for hanging

Attach screw eyes and wire to the back of the girl's head for hanging (see Preparing a Mosaic for Hanging, page 19). Either hang the body beneath it in the same manner or, if you'd prefer, prop it up against the wall, as shown on page 108.

She
lived
vicariously
through
no one.

Materials

11" × 14" (28cm × 36cm) plywood panel

Pencil

Acrylic paints in the following colors: flesh, turquoise, red, yellow and white

Assortment of paintbrushes

Oil pastels

Mixed-media elements such as newspaper, magazine pages and scrapbook embellishments

Computer and printer

Photo-editing software such as Adobe Photoshop

Glue stick

Two-part epoxy resin

Embossing heat tool

Craft sticks

13" × 16" (33cm × 41cm) wooden frame

Mirror

Glass scorer

Running pliers

Tile adhesive

Beige grout

Scissors

Plastic trash bags

Disposable cups

Towel

She Said

DON'T WE ALL YEARN FOR THE PERFECT LIFE? WHAT is a "perfect" life for you? Life is a never-ending journey for me. Every day I learn more about how to go with the flow, accept things for the way they are, live in the moment and strive for excellence. I feel blessed with each new beginning that life provides for me.

This project is an abstract self-portrait and a mixed-media mosaic. I loved recycling old magazines and small scraps of paper by using them in this collage, which I then finished with epoxy resin. The frame is covered with pieces of mirror, but you could change the design to suit your style by substituting tiles, glass or broken crockery to make a different sort of mosaic.

"Try as hard as we may for perfection, the net result of our labors is an amazing variety of imperfectedness. We are surprised at our own versatility in being able to fail in so many different ways."

—Samuel McChord Crothers

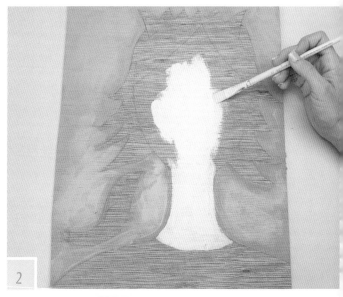

1 Draw design
Outline the basic elements of your design on the plywood board with a pencil.

2 Paint background elements
Paint the largest elements of the collage with acrylic paints. If desired, begin layering colors. Allow the paint to dry completely.

3 Add mixed-media elements
Begin layering mixed-media elements in the background of the collage. Here, I drew swirls over the background in white oil pastels. I then added circles of newspaper and further decorated them with oil pastels and acrylic paints.

Open a picture of yourself in a photo-editing program. Crop the eyes, nose and mouth from the picture. Print the separate images of your features. Cut out each feature and, using a glue stick, glue it to the face on the collage. Cut out images of hair from magazine pages to use for the hair on the collage.

4 Continue embellishing
Create clothes for the figure in your collage with decorative papers and scrapbook embellishments. Use your computer's word processor to type and print out a phrase for your collage. I used a phrase that I wrote: "She lived vicariously through no one." Cut out the words and adhere them to your collage with a glue stick. Finish decorating the collage with oil pastels and acrylic paints.

5

5 Apply epoxy

Protect your work area with plastic trash bags. Elevate the piece above the work surface with several disposable cups. Mix the two-part epoxy resin following the manufacturer's instructions (see Using a Two-Part Epoxy Resin, pages 20–21).

Pour the epoxy over the surface of the project, starting in the center. Spread the epoxy to cover the entire surface of the piece in an even layer, allowing any excess coating to run off the edges of the piece. Scrape the edges with a craft stick to eliminate any drips.

Eliminate bubbles in the epoxy with an embossing heat tool. Allow the epoxy to completely cure, following the manufacturer's guidelines.

6 Tile frame

Using a glass scorer and running pliers, cut the mirror into 1" × ½" (3cm × 1cm) pieces. Adhere the pieces to the front and the edges of the wooden frame with tile adhesive. Allow the adhesive to dry completely.

7 Grout frame

Mix red acrylic paint with beige grout and grout the frame, including the front and the edges (see Using Grout, page 18). Clean the tiles once the grout has set. Once the surface is smooth, buff the tesserae with a clean towel. Allow the grout to dry completely.

8 Frame collage

Secure the collage inside of the tile frame with tile adhesive. Allow the glue to dry completely.

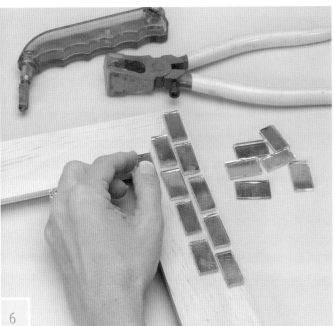

6

7

8

Patterns

Art Is Life, page 28.
Enlarge pattern by 175% to bring to full size.

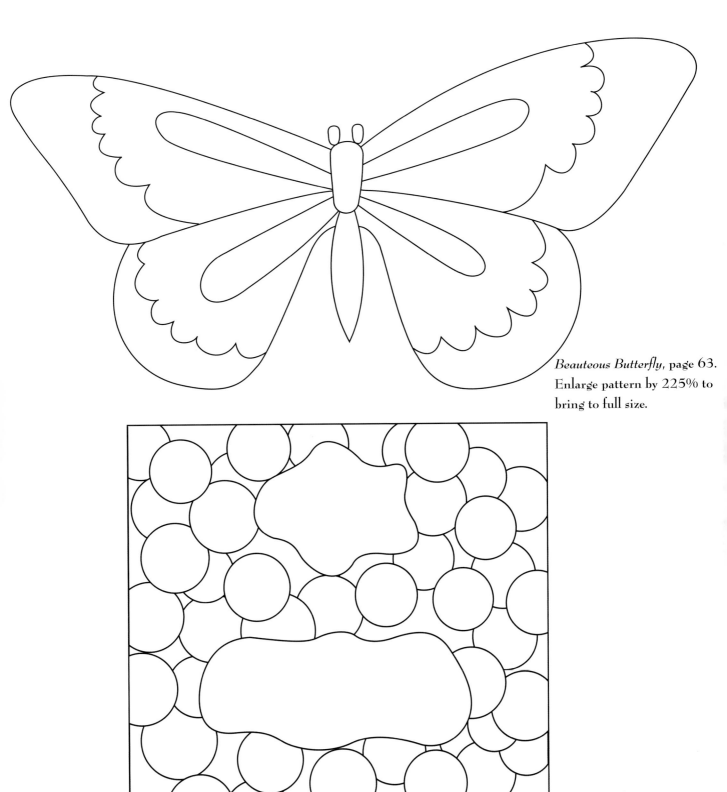

Beauteous Butterfly, page 63.
Enlarge pattern by 225% to
bring to full size.

Under the Blue, page 56.
Enlarge pattern by 400%.
Then enlarge again by
150% to bring to full size.

Mystical Mandala, page 48.
Enlarge pattern by 304% to bring to full size.

Give Yourself Wings, page 36.
Enlarge pattern by 151% to bring to full size.

Proud Peacock, page 80.
Enlarge pattern by 400%. Then enlarge again
by 125% to bring to full size.

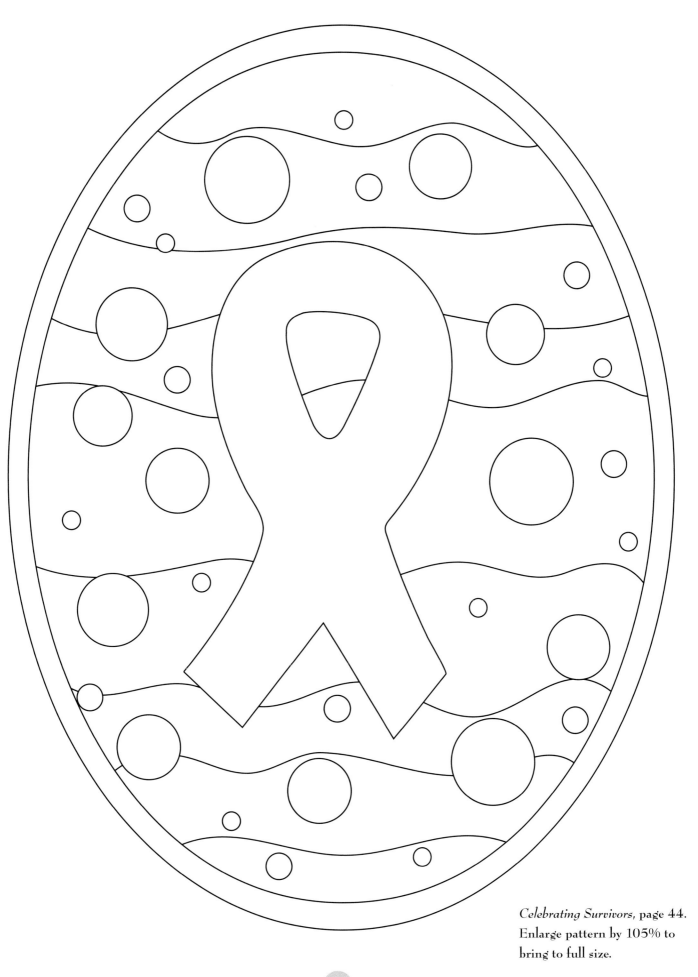

Celebrating Survivors, page 44.
Enlarge pattern by 105% to
bring to full size.

Puzzle Pieces, page 32.
Enlarge pattern by 155% to bring to full size.

Dreams of Degas, page 52.
Enlarge pattern by 400%. The enlarge again by
124% to bring to full size.

Burst of Sunshine, page 74.
Enlarge pattern by 376% to bring to full size.

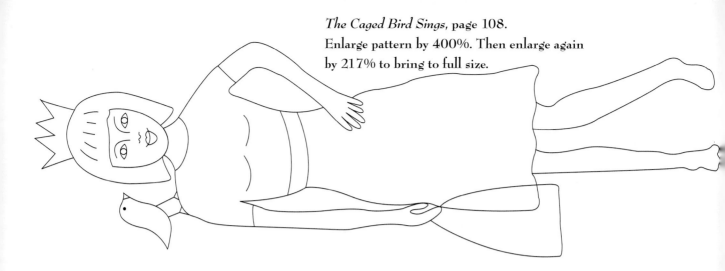

The Caged Bird Sings, page 108.
Enlarge pattern by 400%. Then enlarge again
by 217% to bring to full size.

Resources

When looking for resources for your mosaic work, remember that you can find ways to create and score your tesserae inexpensively. Thrift stores, garage sales and discount shops have great deals on crockery. Tools, supplies and other tesserae are available at your local home improvement stores and craft and hobby stores. The Internet is also a wonderful resource. eBay in particular houses tons of online mosaic retailers, but that's just one of many innovative Web sites providing unique resources for artists and crafters. And, of course, I can't help but mention that there are also some wonderful, talented mosaic artists sharing their techniques in their own inspiring books and Web sites. It would be impossible to name them all, but I've included a few favorites here.

Mosaic Supplies

Mosaic Mercantile
877-966-7242
www.mosaicmercantile.com

Plaid Enterprises, Inc.
800-842-4197
www.plaidonline.com

Society of American Mosaic Artists
www.americanmosaics.org

Weldbond
800-388-2001
www.weldbondusa.com

Wit's End Mosaic
888-494-8736
www.witsendmosaic.com

Inspiring Mosaic Artists

Laurie Mika
www.mikaarts.com

Sonia King
www.mosaicworks.com

Irina Charny
www.icmosaics.com

Laurel True
www.truemosaics.com

Instructions for Laying Tile

The Complete Guide to Masonry & Stonework: Includes Decorative Concrete Treatments (Black & Decker Complete Guide)
Tom Lemmer, Creative Publishing international, September 2006

Ron Hazelton's HouseCalls: How to Make a Tile Patio
www.ronhazelton.com/howto/tile_patio.htm

Index

Check out these other wild titles from North Light Books!

Wild Tiles
by Chrissie Grace
Learn to transform any plain surface into a one-of-a-kind mosaic piece. *Wild Tiles* features 20 projects and a host of variations for creating mosaics with a mixed-media approach. There is a mosaic project here for every skill level, from simple and quick candle holders and mirrors to a large wall-hanging and even a table. In addition to standard tiles and ceramic pieces, these mosaics incorporate painting, polymer clay and even collage. You'll find a helpful glossary of mosaic terms and an invaluable resource guide in the book as well.
ISBN-10: 1-58180-908-5, ISBN-13: 978-1-58180-908-4, paperback, 128 pages, Z0486

Mixed-Media Mosaics
by Laurie Mika
Learn to craft highly textural and vividly colored icons, boxes, tables, items of personal adornment and more using a combination of manufactured and handmade tiles. Step-by-step demos will teach you to make your own polymer clay tiles using techniques such as painting and glazing, stamping, embedding items like beads and buttons, mixing pigments and mica powders with clay, adding metallic leaf and more. Also included are ideas and techniques helpful for personalizing your artwork by adding stamped letters to spell out a special name, or by incorporating ephemera or found objects to commemorate a memorable trip or event.
ISBN-10: 1-58180-983-2 ISBN-13: 978-1-58180-983-1, paperback, 128 pages, Z0823

Garden Mosaics Made Easy
by Jane Pompilio and Cliff Kennedy
Mosaics are a simple, elegant way to enhance the natural beauty of your home and garden. This book features 25 step-by-step mosaic projects featuring ready-to-use design templates. Projects will teach you how to create projects based on a photograph, or how to incorporate memory art into your mosaics. You'll find a wealth of tips on using a wide variety of creative materials such as stained glass, china, pottery, shells and more. The book includes a quick primer on contemporary mosaic techniques such as groutless mosaics and direct and indirect methods of laying tile.
ISBN-13: 978-1-58180-720-2, ISBN-10: 1-58180-720-1, paperback, 128 pages, 33393

These and other fine North Light Books are available at your local craft retailer, bookstore or online supplier, or visit our Web site at **www.mycraftivity.com**.